OSPREY AIRCRAFT OF THE ACES® • 45

# British and Empire Aces of World War 1

SERIES EDITOR: TONY HOLMES

OSPREY AIRCRAFT OF THE ACES® • 45

# British and Empire Aces of World War 1

Christopher Shores

OSPREY
PUBLISHING

**Front cover**
On 27 October 1918 Major W G Barker, the great ace of the Italian Front, was back in France, flying a new Sopwith Snipe. Having shot down a two-seater he became involved in combat with a number of Fokker D.VIIs from an unidentified unit, three of which he was later credited with having shot down, before being shot down himself. Barker was wounded in three places, but survived to be awarded a Victoria Cross

First published in Great Britain in 2001 by Osprey Publishing
Elms Court, Chapel Way, Botley, Oxford, OX2 9LP
E-mail: info@ospreypublishing.com

ISBN 1 84176 377 2

Edited by Mary Orr
Page design by TT Designs, T & B Truscott
Cover Artwork by Keith Woodcock
Aircraft Profiles by Harry Dempsey & Mark Rolfe
Index by Alan Thatcher
Origination by Grasmere Digital Imaging, Leeds, UK
Printed through Bookbuilders, Hong Kong

01  02  03  04  05    10 9 8 7 6 5 4 3 2 1

For a catalogue of all Osprey Publishing titles please contact us at:

**Osprey Direct UK, PO Box 140, Wellingborough, Northants NN8 4ZA, UK**
E-mail: **info@ospreydirect.co.uk**

**Osprey Direct USA, c/o Motorbooks International, 729 Prospect Ave, PO Box 1, Osceola, WI 54020, USA**
E-mail: **info@ospreydirectusa.com**

Or visit our website: **www.ospreypublishing.com**

# CONTENTS

# EARLY DAYS

**W**hen the First World War broke out in August 1914 the concept of a battle in the skies between opposing aircraft was still the stuff of contemporary science fiction. It must be remembered that it was about 12 years since man had first flown in a heavier-than-air craft, and considerably less than that since Louis Blériot had achieved the first non-stop flight across the English Channel. Indeed the wonder is that the inherently conservative military establishments of most of the world's major powers had already seen so great a promise in this new-fangled invention to allocate human and financial resources to acquire and test it for military purposes.

At this stage the aeroplane was seen as no more than a vehicle for reconnaissance, able to trespass further into hostile territory with less risk and effort than could the traditional troop of cavalry. These early machines were without doubt the fragile, unreliable collections of stick and string which have since been classified as representing aviation during this first air war. However, the development of aviation during the four years which followed proved to be rapid in the extreme. This earlier description, whilst perhaps apt for 1914–15, is inappropriate and unfair when considering the machines of 1917–18. By that time the aircraft in front line service were tough, robust, and remarkably reliable. Further, the essential doctrines of aerial warfare had already been developed to a degree

An enlisted man who later became an officer – and the most highly decorated British ace – James McCudden is seen here in the rear seat of one of No 3 Squadron's Deperdussin monoplanes while still a pre-war First Class Air Mechanic *(Bruce Robertson)*

Five years later, Major James McCudden is pictured in the cockpit of his powerful new Royal Aircraft Factory S.E.5 fighter. McCudden was killed in a take-off accident in July 1918 *(MARS)*

of considerable sophistication and effectiveness. Indeed, much that had been learned and put into effect during 1918 was rapidly forgotten or pushed aside in the years of peace which followed. The reasons for this were partly fiscal, but much to do with the efforts of the protagonists of air power to keep their new services free of becoming mere adjuncts to the older services. The consequence was that many of these well-founded lessons had to be relearned at considerable cost during World War 2.

During the early months of the Great War, as World War 1 came to be called, those small numbers of aircraft available rapidly showed their value in the reconnaissance role, establishing their credentials with the powers-that-be. As the front line stabilised across Western Europe, however, their spheres of activity narrowed, and soon the machines of the opposing sides were encountering each other in the air. Initially, it has often been recorded, little more than a casual wave of the hand to the opposition was given. That state of affairs did not last for long. This was war, and the pilots and observers involved were young and aggressive. Rapidly they began employing rifles and revolvers to take potshots at their opposite numbers, also taking into the air with them grenades, metal darts, or any other weapon they could find which they might then drop from the air to the discomfort of those in the trenches below.

It so happened that the development of the aircraft had followed quite close on the heels of that of the machine gun. Even prior to the war experiments had been undertaken by several nations, including Great Britain, to fit such a weapon in the nose of a pusher-type aircraft. Such experiments had essentially been with a view to employing such weaponry against targets on the ground. With only low-powered engines available, coupled with the weight of the water-cooled guns such as the Maxim or the Vickers, the loss of performance occasioned to the aircraft then available appeared unacceptable. Lighter, air-cooled guns and more powerful engines would first be necessary.

Both were appearing by 1914, and for the Royal Flying Corps (RFC) the relatively lightweight Lewis machine gun offered new opportunities. It was not long before a pilot had one such weapon mounted on his two-seater

One of the first British aircraft capable of even the most limited use in the fighter role was the Sopwith Tabloid, here illustrated by a machine delivered to No 5 Squadron of the Royal Flying Corps in May 1914. Pilots of fast and nimble aircraft such as this often carried revolvers which they would empty at a German machine, or a box of steel flechettes that they would empty over German troop concentrations. Nos 3 and 4 Squadrons operated the Tabloid over the Western Front in the first stages of the war *(Bruce Robertson)*

A 7.7 mm (0.303 in) Lewis gun was mounted on a quadrant mounting over the upper wing of several Allied fighters (including the Nieuport Nie.17 as seen here with 'Billy' Bishop in the cockpit). This allowed the gun to be pulled back and down so that the ammunition drum could be changed, but was also favoured by pilots such as Albert Ball for firing upward and forward into the lower fuselage of an unsuspecting enemy aeroplane (MARS)

machine for the observer to operate when he attempted to intercept a German aircraft appearing regularly to reconnoitre his airfield. The weight still affected performance too much, however, and he was ordered to remove the gun. But the possibility had been proven and as more powerful and reliable aircraft began to arrive at the front it became accepted practice to fit a movable machine gun for use by the observer. At first the reason was defensive, rather than offensive, allowing the crew to complete their reconnaissance or artillery spotting flight without interference.

Even at the start of the war most air forces possessed a few fast, light, single-seater aircraft, which were initially employed for high speed scouting behind enemy lines. These relied on their speed and manoeuvrability for their safety. Since no observer was carried, there was no provision for armament either. The higher performance offered by such machines soon persuaded some of their pilots that they offered an opportunity to intercept the enemy's two-seaters and at the least disrupt them from their tasks and drive them off, or even inflict damage or casualty. Some pilots therefore began to experiment, for instance strapping one or two cut-down carbines to the interplane struts of their aircraft to offer a degree of offensive potential.

The majority of such early 'scouts' were tractor aeroplanes (i.e. with the engine at the front, pulling the aircraft through the air). Thus the presence of the propeller in front of the pilot prevented his having a clear field of fire in the direction that would allow him to employ his weapons to greatest effect and accuracy. It became abundantly clear at an early date that to be able to point the aircraft at the chosen target and then fire the gun on this axis offered by far the greatest opportunity of success.

The problem posed was not seen as insoluble, even initially, for many of the Allied two-seaters in use at

These two 7.7 mm (0.303 in) weapons were the two most important aircraft guns operated by the Allies in World War 1. Seen in its ground-based form in the upper photograph, the Lewis gun was a gas-operated weapon supplied with ammunition from a 47-round single-row or 97-round twin-row drum magazine, and in its aerial form was modified with a spade grip rather than a stocked butt and also with the barrel and gas cylinder radiator either removed or replaced by a light aluminium casing. The Vickers gun was revised with air rather than water cooling (typified by a louvered air-cooling casing in place of the ground-based weapon's water-cooling jacket) and was supplied with ammunition from a belt drawn from a magazine in the fuselage (Bruce Robertson)

8

this time were 'pusher' aircraft, with the engine behind the pilot and the propeller at the rear, as on a ship. In such aircraft the observer sat in front of the pilot to allow him the clearest possible view of the ground. He was thus also offered the potential for a clear forward shot with his defensive weapon. The fact that this was flexibly mounted at first appeared to offer an additional advantage, allowing fire to be continued at an opponent in front who was seeking to curve away, climb or dive.

## ENTER THE WARPLANE

The first British aircraft designed with specific offensive activities in mind was just such a 'pusher' two-seater, the Vickers F.B.5, which rapidly became known as the 'Gun-bus'. The first examples of this aircraft arrived in France in February 1915 and were issued to No 5 Squadron, RFC, providing that service with an early advantage over the German Air Service. The first victory over an enemy aircraft by the crew of one of these machines was gained during May.

The next series of developments which had significant effects on the appearance of the true fighter aircraft were achieved by the French and Germans. Like the British, the French at this time had received a number of single-seat scouting aircraft, offering potential for offensive deployment. Most of these were of Morane design and manufacture, and were of a monoplane configuration. During March 1915 the first *escadrilles* were formed with the Type 'L' aircraft, which had a machine gun (usually a Hotchkiss light air-cooled weapon) mounted on the forward fuselage immediately in front of the pilot. This gun was so mounted as to fire at an angle, above the arc of the propeller. This was not a successful adaptation, as aiming and firing with any degree of accuracy proved to be extremely difficult.

A month later a well-known pre-war aviator, Roland Garros, who was serving with *Escadrille* MS23, mounted a Hotchkiss to fire directly forward, having tapered wedges of armour plate fitted to the inside faces of the propeller blades to deflect any bullets which might strike these blades when the gun was fired. The installation was a crude and dangerous attempt to permit direct forward fire, and frequently damaged the blades and threw the engine out of alignment. Nonetheless, when it worked, it

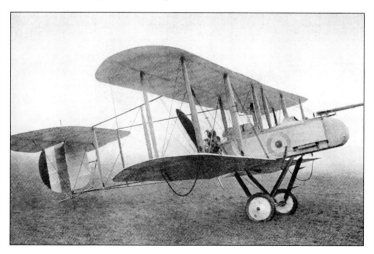

Before the introduction of the synchronised gun which could fire forward through the airscrew, an early British fighting biplane, the Vickers F.B.5 'Gun-bus', did good service in 1915. The gunner, armed with a Lewis gun, had to sit in front of the pilot in the nose of the nacelle

9

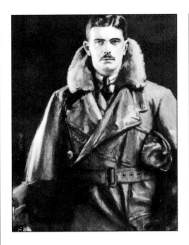

On 7 November 1915 Lieutenant
G S M Insall, flying a Vickers F.B.5
'Gun-bus' of No 11 Squadron, forced
down an Aviatik two-seater with
his aggressive flying and then
destroyed the aeroplane on the
ground with an incendiary bomb.
Insall was awarded the VC on
23 December of the same year
*(Bruce Robertson)*

Temporary Major Lanoe Hawker
was the first 'fighter pilot' to receive
the Victoria Cross, for bravery in the
air on 25 July 1915

proved quite effective, and during the first half of April Garros shot down
three German aircraft and damaged others, causing great concern in the
opposing air service.

Sadly for Garros, the unreliability of his device proved its own
downfall, and on 19 April 1915 he was obliged to force-land in German-
held territory when his engine failed. Although he attempted to destroy
his machine, he was captured. The Germans were immediately aware that
they had inadvertently come into possession of the scourge of their
reconnaissance aircraft, and passed the wreckage to Dutch aircraft
designer Anthony Fokker in order that copies might be manufactured.

Fokker's engineers at once observed the limitations of Garros's
modifications, but they were aware that systems for the mechanical
interruption of a machine gun to allow it to fire through the revolving
propeller arc had already been designed and patented. At once they
produced their own version of such a device, whereby the revolutions of a
cam actuated by the engine prevented the gun from firing when the blades
of the propeller were directly in line with the muzzle of the gun. This was
the first true interruption system to be constructed and tested, and it was at
once fitted to one of Fokker's own monoplane single-seaters, the M5K(A
III) for demonstration to the German clients. The latter were greatly
impressed, and placed orders for what became the E.I – the first purpose-
built single-seater fighting aircraft to go into production.

The next important development was a British one, for with the
availability of more aircraft with offensive capabilities on both sides of the
lines, aerial engagements began to escalate. During May 1915 the
number of Allied reconnaissance aircraft attacked and diverted from their
duties over the Ypres area began to give serious cause for concern. On
14 February 1915 No 11 Squadron, RFC, had been formed, equipped
entirely with Vickers F.B.5s, as the first dedicated fighting unit; it was
now rushed to France for such duties. The French too had sought to
rapidly develop their early experiments with fighting scouts. Some
very promising new biplane aircraft were appearing from the Nieuport
factory, and Lewis guns were fitted to these, above the top wings, firing
directly forward above the propeller arc. Although less accurate to aim
and more difficult to rearm or rectify a jam, than a weapon mounted
directly in front of the pilot, it proved a fair compromise until better
systems could be devised. Two such aircraft were initially produced, the
two-seater Nieuport 10 and the single-seater Nieuport 11, known as the
'Bebe'; both were tractor machines, and the latter was to be the first of a
long line of successful Nieuport Scouts.

Meanwhile one of the first adaptations to create a single-seat fighting
scout for the RFC had occurred when a local field modification to a Bristol
Scout biplane was undertaken in No 6 Squadron, RFC, by Captain L G
Hawker a trained engineer, veteran flyer, and a flight commander in
the unit. Aided by Air Mechanic E J Elton, he designed an attachment
allowing a Lewis gun to be mounted on the side of the fuselage, just ahead
of the cockpit, and to fire forward and outward at such an angle as to just
miss the tips of the propeller. Although possessing similar disadvantages to
the early French systems, Hawker did manage to achieve some early success
with this aircraft, and on 25 July 1915 he twice engaged German aircraft,
shooting one down in flames and driving down two others. For these

actions and previous good work he was awarded the Victoria Cross, the first 'fighter pilot' to be so honoured.

By this time No 6 Squadron had received a few examples of a new two-seater 'pusher' biplane, similar in general arrangement to the F.B.5 'Gun-bus', but of somewhat higher performance. This was the Royal Aircraft Factory F.E.2b, first of a long and distinguished line of aircraft which were to serve with the RFC, and subsequently with the Royal Air Force (RAF), throughout the rest of the war. In July 1915 the type was not yet generally available, but in one of these early examples, with a gunner in the front cockpit, Hawker gained several more victories during the summer, and became the RFC's first 'ace'. He was closely followed by Captain L W B Rees of No 11 Squadron, the most successful exponent of the Vickers F.B.5, who claimed his sixth success in one of these aircraft on the last day of October 1915, and by Captain C G Bell of No 10 Squadron, who also achieved some success with a modified Bristol Scout, claiming his fifth victory at the end of November. It is also interesting to note that Lanoe Hawker's able assistant, Elton, subsequently trained as a pilot and became a successful air fighter in his own right.

Britain also possessed a Royal Naval Air Service (RNAS) at this time, and this too had been developing armed scouts, experimenting with machine gun-armed Sopwith Tabloid biplanes and acquiring a small number of Sopwith-designed 'Gun-buses'. This service utilised its first armed scouts in action in the Dardanelles, initially employing some French-built Nieuport 11s during July 1915, followed the next month by some Bristol Scouts, armed in a similar manner, with top wing Lewis guns.

On the Western Front in France during July the first of the new Fokker E.Is appeared, being issued in small numbers to various *Felfliegerabteilungen* to provide escort to the preponderant reconnaissance

**The gunners of the F.E.2b fought many duels with German airmen from this exposed and precarious position**

The Austin-Ball A.F.B.1 was an experimental fighter that was designed in the spring of 1916 and embodied some of the ideas of 2nd Lieutenant Albert Ball (one of the Royal Flying Corps' rising aces of the period) about what would make a good fighter in terms of armament, performance, and fields of vision for the pilot (*Bruce Robertson*)

machines. The first success with one of these aircraft was actually achieved by Leutnant Kurt Wintgens on 1 July, just a few days after Lanoe Hawker's first victory with the Bristol Scout.

The E.I proved to be rather a poor aircraft in service, but rapid developments allowed the improved E.II and E.III to follow in August and September respectively. At this stage aerial fighting remained infrequent, but already the desirability of grouping fighting scouts into larger, more specialised units, as the British and French were already doing, was becoming obvious to the Germans as well. Such grouping would allow control of the air to be achieved and exercised over specific areas, both to give general protection to friendly aircraft in such areas, and to challenge the larger formations of Allied aircraft which were now beginning to appear. Three *Kampfeinsitzer Kommando* (KEK) were therefore formed, equipped entirely with Fokker monoplanes, and at once proved successful. Losses amongst RFC units rose alarmingly late in the year, and the period subsequently known as the 'Fokker Scourge' had begun.

Once available to operate in numbers, the Fokkers proved too fast and manoeuvrable for No 11 Squadron's 'Gun-buses' to cope with, and by November these aircraft were clearly outclassed. A replacement was sought, but was not yet available in sufficient quantity. No 18 Squadron had just reached France, but this unit too had been equipped with the F.B.5; it was not until April 1916 that this squadron received the more potent F.E.2b. Meanwhile however, No 20 Squadron, which had been formed with these new aircraft, was rushed through training and dispatched to France with all haste, arriving on 23 January 1916. During the same month the French were also able to form the first *escadrille* to be fully equipped with Nieuport 11s – *Escadrille* N3.

The sturdy Sopwith Camel was one of the most successful fighters of World War 1 as a result of its adequate firepower and performance in combination with extraordinary agility. These are aircraft of No 208 Squadron led by Major C Draper, a 12-victory ace who later became known as 'The Mad Major' for a number of post-war feats including flights under several of London's bridges (*Bruce Robertson*)

# 1916: CLASH OF WINGS

T he year 1916 saw air fighting become a serious art. It began badly for the Allied air services as the initiative which they had possessed so firmly during 1915 was inexorably wrested from them by their opponents. In an effort to reduce losses the RFC issued an interim order that each reconnaissance aircraft must be escorted over the front by at least three other aircraft for the time being.

By now production of a new single-seater fighting scout designed by Geoffrey de Havilland, and known as the Airco D.H.2, was underway in England. De Havilland had been responsible for the design of the F.E.2 series, and the new aircraft was of somewhat similar concept in that it was a 'pusher' biplane, not dependent upon the still non-available interrupter gear for the machine gun. The pilot sat in a fuselage nacelle in front of the engine, manning the controls and a forward-firing Lewis gun. The latter was provided with a limited amount of traverse and elevation, although in practice pilots rapidly discovered that it was better to clamp this in the fixed position, allowing the whole aircraft simply to be aimed at the target, as was to become the norm with all fighting scouts in the immediate future. Initially, however, this modification was immediately forbidden by the authorities, who, of course, believed that they knew better than the pilots at the front!

No 24 Squadron, led by Major Hawker, VC, DSO, arrived in France with the first of these new aircraft early in February 1916, followed during March by the similarly-equipped No 29 Squadron. More F.E.2bs also

**The Germans found out all about the agile Airco D.H.2 when a prototype being flown by No 5 Squadron RFC fell into their hands soon after arriving in France (Bruce Robertson)**

A little known British ace of No 24 Squadron, Captain I D R McDonald was awarded the MC and DFC, and his final tally was 20 victories (*Bruce Robertson*)

The Martinsyde G.100 'Elephant' had a short life as a fighter before being relegated to long-range bombing duties. This is the prototype, first flown in September 1915

became available, with No 25 Squadron reaching France in February, No 23 Squadron in March and No 22 Squadron in April. These new aircraft, joined by the French Nieuports, quickly regained the initiative against the Fokkers, which despite their effective armament proved to have a rather disappointing performance. Once all the new Allied units were established in action, superiority in the air was regained.

During March 1916 another single-seater type arrived over the front with the RFC's No 27 Squadron. Known as the 'Elephant', due to its large and rather cumbersome size and appearance, the Martinsyde G.100 was a tractor biplane with a top wing Lewis gun firing above the propeller arc, similar to the installation on the Nieuports. Designed as a reconnaissance machine rather than a fighting scout, it nonetheless proved quite effective against its initial opposition, gaining some success with No 27 Squadron during its early days of service, some dozen or so pilots claiming victories whilst flying it. It rapidly became outclassed however, and although it was later to serve with several other units, it was relegated to long-range bombing duties as soon as more effective machines became available.

Whilst all these new units were beginning to arrive in France, the Germans undertook their first substantial concentration of fighting scouts in the Verdun area, where the French were commencing a large-scale offensive on the ground. Here *Kampfeinsitzer Kommando Sud* and *Nord* gained some quite remarkable successes, Leutnant Oswald Boelcke rising swiftly to prominence as the leading fighting pilot of the German Air Service at this time.

Meanwhile in England another breakthrough was occurring. The RFC continued with all speed to form further units of aircraft capable of dealing with the Fokker monoplanes, but engineers had also pressed on with work on a reliable interrupter gear. Fokker's design had been a mechanical solution, activated by cams and rods linked to the

The Bristol Scout was a British aeroplane that saw limited use as an extemporised fighter. This is a Scout C seen at the Royal Naval Air Service's establishment on the Isle of Grain in northern Kent. When armament was carried the original types of mounting – designed to fire forward and outward past the circumference of the propeller disc – were replaced by one, or very occasionally two, fixed forward-firing Lewis guns above the upper-wing centre section. The last few aircraft had a Vickers synchronised machine gun in the upper part of the forward fuselage *(Bruce Robertson)*

engine. The British, however, sought to further develop a hydraulic system invented by a Rumanian engineer, Constantinescu. Employing this approach, they fitted a Vickers machine gun above the engine cowling of a Bristol Scout during March, sending this aircraft to France for urgent trials. Initially much trouble was experienced, but the installation showed promise and development continued with all haste.

During April 1916 the RNAS introduced a new two-seater tractor biplane to service in France, which joined 5 Wing at Coudekerque, on the Channel coast. Known in service as the Sopwith 1½ Strutter, it was initially armed only with a Lewis gun for the observer to allow it to operate in the reconnaissance and bombing roles. However, so excellent was the performance it offered that it was chosen to be the first British aircraft to be fitted with a forward-firing Vickers gun above the engine as soon as production of the improved Constantinescu interrupter gear allowed. So fitted, it was able to operate either as a fighter, or in its designed role, although the RNAS were also having a single-seat version produced as a dedicated bombing aircraft.

Initially the new Sopwith provided escort to No 5 Wing's more numerous Breguet V and Caudron G.4 bombers, but the aircraft's performance was so outstanding that a number were transferred to the RFC, No 70 Squadron beginning formation before the end of April to become a two-seat fighting unit. The first flight moved to France as early as 24 May, followed during the next two months by the rest of the unit as training and equipping was completed.

Even as all these new types reached France, the need for every available fighting scout saw the arrival in France, late in May, of No 60 Squadron. Sent over without aircraft, the unit was to equip with whatever could be acquired from the French, which turned out to be a variety of Morane-

Saulnier types. Type N 'Bullet' monoplanes went to one flight, whilst Type BB biplanes and Type L and LA parasol monoplanes equipped the other flights – although these latter aircraft were quickly replaced by more Type Ns.

The Nieuport company was at this time rapidly developing the successful Type 11, and before the spring was through the RFC purchased a number of these aircraft, and also the new Type 13 and Type 16 Scouts, which were issued to No 11 and No 29 Squadrons to augment their existing equipment. During May the most famous and numerous of the Nieuport Scouts appeared at the front with the French *Escadrille* N57; this was the Type 17, a few of which were soon also in British hands. The Type 17 was supplied to No 1 Squadron to operate alongside that unit's two-seaters.

Additionally at this time a very limited number of Bristol Scouts armed with top wing Lewis guns reached No 11 and No 25 Squadrons, while a third unit of D.H.2s, No 32 Squadron led by Major L W B Rees, also arrived in France during May.

A notable engagement occurred over the front on 29 April 1916, when Lord Doune, a pilot in No 25 Squadron (who did not become an ace), with Lieutenant R V Walker as his gunner, shot down a Fokker monoplane of *Fliegerabteilung* 18, which proved to have been flown by a fellow nobleman, the son of Prinz Ernst von Sachsen-Meingen. By this time the 'Fokker Scourge' was fast approaching its end, and by June 1916 the RFC's force of fighting scouts available on the Western Front had been very considerably expanded.

The RFC now gained further support from the RNAS, when during the early summer this service formed a fighting unit to be known initially as 'A' Squadron. Based at Furnes, this unit was to be responsible for the defence of the Channel coast supply ports, and saw a fair amount of action in this role. It was also used for the operational testing by the Admiralty of new scout types which were being ordered into production.

As the summer approached, with the prospect of better weather, the British planned a huge offensive on the Somme Front. By now the ascendancy which had been regained by the RFC was marked by a notable success. During an engagement between No 25 Squadron's F.E.2bs and

The Nieuport Nie.12 was a two-seat reconnaissance fighter used operationally in modest numbers, together with the differently engined Nie.20, by Nos 1, 45 and 46 Squadrons in France and by No 39 Squadron for home defence *(MARS)*

The Royal Aircraft Factory F.E.2d was a large and fairly cumbersome two-seat biplane operated as a multi-role type. As a 'fighter', the F.E.2d was armed with three or four 7.7 mm (0.303 in) Lewis guns, one on a trainable mounting in the front cockpit, one or two on fixed forward-firing mountings for use by the pilot in the rear cockpit, and the last on a trainable telescopic mounting between the cockpits to fire over the upper wing in a fashion that required the gunner to stand up in the front cockpit. J T B McCudden flew the type for a short time with No 20 Squadron before being transferred to No 29 Squadron who operated the Airco D.H.2 fighter *(Bruce Robertson)*

some Fokker monoplanes on 18 June, Corporal J H Waller, the gunner in 2nd Lieutenant G R McCubbin's aircraft, shot down and killed the first great German ace of the war, Leutnant Max Immelmann, who was still second only to Boelcke. McCubbin was another pilot not destined to become an ace himself.

Later that same month the Nieuport Scout units launched a series of attacks against the German observation balloon lines prior to the launching of the offensive on the ground. These heavily defended targets were attacked with le Prieur rockets, mounted on the interplane struts of the Nieuports, which were fired electrically. In two days eight balloons had been destroyed in flames.

Reinforcement and re-equipment continued as rapidly as possible, and by the end of June the Royal Aircraft Factory F.E.2d, a development of the F.E. design equipped with a new 250 hp engine, started to reach France, going in the first instance to No 20 Squadron. The first examples of a new single-seater 'pusher' of very similar appearance to the Airco D.H.2 also arrived. This aircraft, the F.E.8, was issued first to No 29 Squadron, replacing that unit's few Nieuport 16s, and operating alongside the preponderant D.H.2s.

The Somme Offensive commenced on 1 July, on which date the RFC fielded some 81 single-seater scouts, although only six of these were Nieuport 17s – considered generally to be the best aircraft available. On this opening day Major L W B Rees of No 32 Squadron made a single-handed attack on ten German two-seaters for which he was awarded the Victoria Cross.

The offensive brought considerable activity in the air, the new Sopwiths of No 70 Squadron particularly achieving a number of successes, especially whilst engaged in escorting the Martinsyde 'Elephants' of No 27 Squadron on bombing raids. The Nieuports were also very active, and a young Lieutenant with No 11 Squadron named Albert Ball was starting to build up a good number of claims whilst flying these aircraft. D.H.2s remained

This Albatros D.I fighter of the *Jasta Boelcke's* Leutnant Buettner was forced down behind the British lines on 1 December 1916. Repaired and revised with British rather than German markings, the aeroplane was used for evaluation, one of the pilots who flew it being J T B McCudden *(Bruce Robertson)*

at the fore, and on 21 July No 24 Squadron claimed nine victories out of 25 hostile aircraft encountered during two engagements. Captain A M Wilkinson was pre-eminent at this time and by the end of August he had become the most successful exponent of this aircraft, with ten victories to his credit.

Despite these successes, No 60 Squadron's Moranes had proved very vulnerable, and so heavy were losses that by mid August it had become necessary to remove this unit from the front to re-form. To do this, the Nieuport Scouts and their pilots from No 11 Squadron were transferred to this unit, No 11 re-equipping fully with F.E.2bs.

Although the RFC was by now well in control, the demand for more scouts was increasing, and another new type was about to become available. The 'new' aircraft was not a success however. The B.E.12 was simply a single-seater version of the inherently stable B.E.2c reconnaissance aircraft, with a Vickers machine gun attached to the side of the forward fuselage, firing forward with the benefit of an interrupter gear. No 19 Squadron arrived at St Omer with these aircraft during July, whilst No 21 Squadron at Fienvillers replaced its two-seater R.E.7s with them. This latter experienced unit gained a few early successes with the aircraft, but basically it proved a complete failure. A few were supplied to No 17 Squadron in the Middle East to supplement its B.E.2s, this unit also receiving a few Bristol Scout Ds and Nieuport Scouts at this time to allow a fighter flight to be formed in this area. Other B.E.12s were retained in England for home defence against Zeppelin raids. The only pilot to achieve anything of note with the ill-fated B.E.12 was No 17 Squadron's Captain G W Murlis-Green who made six claims whilst flying these aircraft.

The first full unit of F.E.8s, No 40 Squadron, reached France during August following delays in introducing the aircraft fully to front line service due to technical teething troubles. Meanwhile, at the end of July the Sopwith 1½ Strutters of No 3 Naval Wing had moved far south into the French area of the front line to undertake strategic bombing attacks over Germany.

The Germans had been quick to analyse the renewed Allied success and sought to counter this. Three new biplane scouts had rapidly been developed to replace the increasingly ineffective Fokker Eindeckers. The first of these, the Fokker D.III, was powered by an air-cooled rotary engine, whilst the other two, the Halberstadt D.II and the Albatros D.I, were fitted with water-cooled power units. The Fokker and Halberstadt machines generally carried a single forward-firing machine gun (some Fokkers were fitted with two), but the Albatros carried two such guns as standard equipment – a notable improvement in fire power.

New fighting units were also now formed, known as *Jagdstaffeln (Jasta)*, the first of these to reach the front being *Jasta* 2, commanded by Oswald Boelcke. The latter claimed his 20th victory on 2 September, and 15 days later he led his unit into action as a whole for the first time during the Battle of Flers-Courcelette. The results were extremely ominous for the RFC; of eight B.E.2s of No 12 Squadron and six F.E.2bs of No 11 Squadron which were encountered, two of the former and four of the latter were shot down, one of these victories falling to Manfred von Richthofen – at that time new to scout flying, but soon to become renowned as the 'Red Baron', probably the world's most famous fighter pilot. By September Boelcke's personal total had reached 29, and it was becoming obvious that the RFC's period of supremacy was facing a serious challenge – particularly the B.E.12 squadrons.

Development was also proceeding rapidly in England. As the autumn arrived a unit forming part of what was known as the Dover Defence Flight of the RNAS, No 2 Naval Squadron, was supplied with a new Sopwith Scout, which rapidly received the unofficial name of 'Pup'. A delightful aircraft to fly, the new Pup represented the cutting edge of British design at the time; a tractor biplane with a rotary engine, fitted with a single forward-firing Vickers gun, it was both fast and nimble. Supplied also to No 1 Naval Wing at Dunkerque, it joined Nieuports which had also been provided to that unit, and was quickly sent into action. Here it displayed its capabilities in convincing style, pilots flying this new aircraft claiming eight victories between 24 September and 30 October.

The Sopwith was clearly superior to the new Fokker D.III, which rapidly disappeared from the front, and the equal of the new Halberstadt and Albatros scouts. The pilots of the RFC were soon clamouring for this aircraft.

Meanwhile, two further RFC units had reached the front. One of these was No 41 Squadron, equipped with F.E.8s, which were already rapidly

The Sopwith Pup, so named as a result of the impression it gave of being the offspring of the 1¹/₂ Strutter, was one of the first truly successful British fighters. The type entered service in the late summer of 1916 and, though armed with just one 7.7 mm (0.303 in) synchronised machine gun, proved itself an outstanding air combat fighter as a result of its agility *(Bruce Robertson)*

becoming obsolete; the other was No 45 Squadron, with Sopwith 1¹/₂ Strutters. Although the latter was now somewhat outclassed by the Albatros D.I, and certainly by the D.II which was already following it into service, 45 Squadron became the most successful unit to fly these aircraft, claiming 88 victories during the next 11 months. No less than 13 of these were credited to Lieutenant G H Cock and his gunners before he was himself shot down and became a PoW during July 1917.

At this time too the French commenced the introduction of a new scout – the SPAD S.VII. This aircraft, which featured a water-cooled engine and a single machine gun, quickly began to replace the Nieuports in the premier *escadrilles de chasse*. A SPAD was tested by No 60 Squadron, but as the British were intending to equip their Nieuport units with other types from England in the near future, no initial order for these aircraft was placed, and in consequence the Nieuport soldiered on for somewhat longer with the RFC.

The Nieuport Nie.17 was a trim sesquiplane fighter not used in large numbers by the British but much favoured by pilots who preferred agility to outright performance and heavy firepower. Many celebrated 'balloon busting' pilots flew the type *(Bruce Robertson)*

Despite the presence of the new higher-performance German scouts, the two-seater 1¹/2 Strutters and the F.E.2ds managed to continue to hold their own, due mainly to the presence of the observer/gunners with their flexible machine guns. At this time, however, the D.H.2s, F.E.8s and B.E.12s, and the older Corps reconnaissance types (mainly the B.E.2s) began to suffer severely at the hands of the new *Jastas*. Only the Nieuport 17s and the Sopwith Pups were able to challenge on anything approaching equal terms.

Despite this, the Germans still suffered some heavy casualties at times, and on 28 October they lost their greatest ace to date. Two days earlier Oswald Boelcke had claimed his 40th success, but now, as he prepared to engage D.H.2s of No 24 Squadron, he collided with a fellow pilot and fell to his death. As they had done on the occasion of Immelmann's death, the RFC dropped a laurel wreath as tribute to the demise of a gallant foe.

At this time the RFC's own 'star', Albert Ball, had claimed his 31st success, but was about to be sent home for a rest. In England at the age of 20 he was lionised by the Press – the first British pilot to receive such public adulation. This was not surprising, for whilst the French and the Germans had realised quickly the propaganda value to be gained by publicising the exploits of their outstanding pilots, and the extent to which public support and interest in the air services could thereby be enhanced, such an approach was quite outside the ethos of the British services. Thus whilst names such as Boelcke, von Richthofen and the great French ace, Georges Guynemer, became national heroes and household names, the British authorities endeavoured wherever possible not to release similar information. Only when some event such as the award of a Victoria Cross or other high award made publicity inevitable, did the public become aware of names. Essentially, whenever possible the RFC – and to an even greater extent the RNAS, child as it was of the Silent Service – remained nameless services to the public at large.

The Sopwith 1¹/2 Strutter initially had the edge in combat but was soon overtaken by the German Albatros and Halberstadt scouts. Nevertheless it saw extended service with the Royal Naval Air Service. Standing in front of a Sopwith 1¹/2 Strutter in 1916, Flight Sub-Lieutenant J J Malone was a Canadian national who achieved 20 victories with No 3 Squadron of the RNAS *(Bruce Robertson)*

The losses of the B.E.12 units had been so catastrophic, that during September 1916 General Trenchard was obliged to order them to cease operating as fighters and to fly instead as bombers in order to prevent their total annihilation. The RFC had become so concerned regarding the extent of the superiority that the Germans were establishing at this time, that a request was made to the Navy for assistance. Fortunately this was readily forthcoming, for the RNAS had been undertaking a programme of expansion of its fighting scouts, and during the final two months of the year several new units were formed, mostly from within existing formations.

At Furnes 'A' Squadron now became No 1 Naval Squadron, equipped initially with Nieuport 17s and Bristol Scout Cs, whilst at Dunkerque's St Pol airfield the similarly-equipped 'C' Squadron became No 3 Naval. At Coudekerque, No 5 Wing's 'A' Squadron, equipped still with 1½ Strutters, became No 4 Naval, while at Dover No 6 Naval was formed, moving across to Petite Synthe in December with Nieuports. Specifically to assist the RFC, No 8 Naval Squadron was formed at St Pol with personnel drawn from No 1, No 4 and No 5 Wings, this unit being equipped with one flight of Nieuports, one of Pups and one of 1½ Strutters. The unit was despatched to Vert Galant on the Western Front during October, where in mid November more Pups replaced the 1½ Strutters; before the year was out the Nieuports had similarly been replaced, and 20 victories had already been claimed. From this point onwards, the Naval scout units played an ever-increasing part in the fighting on the Western Front.

On 18 November 1916 the British Army launched the last of its desperately costly attacks on the Somme front, while five days later the RFC suffered the loss of its first ace when Major Hawker was shot down and killed during a classic dogfight with Manfred von Richthofen, becoming the latter's 11th victory. This action seemed to set the scene for what was to come in the new year of 1917.

Australian ace Lt R S Dallas of No 1 Naval Wing poses by a Nieuport Type 11 'Bebe'. Dallas claimed his first three victories (out of an eventual total of 32) flying Nieuport Scouts in 1916 (*Norman Franks Collection*)

# 1917:
# NO LET UP

The winter of 1916/17 brought a halt to major operations on the ground and in consequence the pressure of aerial activity also slackened. On both sides of the lines the combatants sought to expand the size and quality of their forces – particularly those pertaining to the respective air services, in preparations for the renewed activity which the spring must surely bring.

Late in 1916 the RFC had received its first Sopwith Pups, and these had been supplied to the new No 54 Squadron which arrived in France before the end of December. The unit was followed in January by No 43 Squadron – the third and last of the 1½ Strutter units to be formed. Meanwhile, following its successful introduction to the Western Front, No 8 Naval Squadron now withdrew to St Pol, its place being taken by No 3 Naval. The latter unit had also been re-equipped with Pups, as had No 4 Naval Squadron.

No 8 Naval's withdrawal was to allow its re-equipment with a superb new aircraft – the Sopwith Triplane. This was essentially a Pup with an extra wing added and a more powerful engine. Its only fault was that its armament was still limited to one machine gun, but the manoeuvrability offered by the extra wing was to prove unequalled. Originally designed and built for the Navy, it was initially ordered by both the RNAS and the RFC. However, the British authorities had somewhat belatedly decided to order the SPAD S.VII for both services also, both from the French constructors and by way of licence construction in Britain. In order to rationalise equipment and allow the maximum number of units to be formed and to reach the front in the quickest possible time, an inter-service agreement was negotiated allowing the RNAS to receive all the Triplanes produced, while the RFC took all the SPADs. Consequently both Nos 1 and 8 Naval Squadrons were re-equipped with the new

No 1 Squadron of the Royal Naval Air Service was a major exponent of the Sopwith Triplane, which entered service in February 1917 and enjoyed a short but very successful career. N5454 in the foreground was the mount of R P Minifie, who ended the war as a Captain in the Royal Air Force with 21 victories
(*Bruce Robertson*)

This was the first example of the SPAD S.VII built under licence in the UK by L. Blériot Aeronautics of Brooklands and Mann, Egerton & Co. Ltd of Norwich. Although it had the same sturdiness as its French-built counterpart, the British-built S.VII had inferior performance, including a speed some 19 to 32 km/h (12 to 20 mph) less. The S.VII was flown operationally by Nos 19, 23 and 60 Squadrons over the Western Front, and by 1 and 2 Squadrons in Palestine and Mesopotamia respectively *(Bruce Robertson)*

aircraft during February, the former unit joining No 3 Naval on the Western Front by the middle of that month.

On 8 March another new type appeared in France with the arrival of No 48 Squadron, the first to fly the Bristol F.2A, a new two-seater reconnaissance fighter, soon to be known by all as the Bristol Fighter; the aircraft was designed to undertake a similar role to that of the RFC's 1½ Strutters, but was of notably superior performance. Within four days No 66 Squadron also arrived, equipped with more Pups, while at last No 29 Squadron exchanged its worn and ageing D.H.2s for Nieuport 17s. On 9 March, however, the equally outclassed F.E.8s had suffered a serious defeat when nine of these aircraft from No 40 Squadron were set upon by von Richthofen's *Jasta* 11. Five were shot down and all the rest suffered damage. In consequence this unit too was hastily re-equipped with Nieuports. The only pilot to achieve any degree of success with the outmoded F.E.8 had been Lieutenant E L Benbow who had claimed eight victories whilst flying this aircraft.

It was not just the older types which suffered badly however, for on 5 April six of No 48 Squadron's new Bristol Fighters, led by Capt W Leefe Robinson, VC, were intercepted by Albatros D.IIs from *Jasta* 11, and four, including that flown by the formation leader, were shot down. Because of this easy victory, von Richthofen reported adversely on the new aircraft. This was to prove an error, for it was not the aircraft, but the tactics employed that had been the problem. Leefe Robinson had been

The Bristol F.2A was the first variant of the Fighter to enter service, but only 50 were completed before the advent of the altogether superior F.2B model with a more powerful engine and a number of features to improve fighting capability *(MARS)*

Lieutenant W Leefe Robinson received the Victoria Cross for shooting down a Zeppelin at Cuffley, Hertfordshire, in the early hours of September 3 1916. In April 1917 he was shot down by von Richthofen and taken prisoner. He died in December 1919 shortly after his release

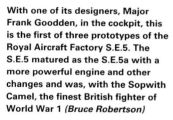

With one of its designers, Major Frank Goodden, in the cockpit, this is the first of three prototypes of the Royal Aircraft Factory S.E.5. The S.E.5 matured as the S.E.5a with a more powerful engine and other changes and was, with the Sopwith Camel, the finest British fighter of World War 1 *(Bruce Robertson)*

until recently a Home Defence pilot, who had been awarded his Victoria Cross for shooting down a Zeppelin by night. He was, however, inexperienced as an air fighter. Against the advice of his fellow flight commanders, including the ex-D.H.2 pilot Alan Wilkinson, he had sought to operate the aircraft as standard reconnaissance two-seaters, rather than seeking to employ their excellent performance to dogfight like single-seaters, but with the added benefit of the rear seat gunners. Further, he had ordered that all oil be removed from the guns to prevent them freezing up in the bitter cold of high altitude in early spring. When attacked, all the gunner's Lewis guns had failed to operate! Leefe Robinson spent the rest of the war as a prisoner, while No 48 Squadron's other flights soon demonstrated how the F.2A *should* be flown.

By this time the German Air Service had increased its establishment to include 37 *Jastas,* the majority now equipped with the Albatros D.II, which was being reinforced by the faster D.III. Although inferior in numbers overall, these units possessed the advantage in performance over the majority of the aircraft facing them. As the British opened the spring campaigning season with the Battle of Arras, the *Jastas* on this front inflicted the heaviest casualties yet sustained by the RFC in what became known as 'Bloody April'; 316 aircrew were lost during this single month.

Better equipment was on the way, albeit more slowly than the units at the front could have wished. On 8 April No 56 Squadron arrived in

Before his death on 7 May 1917, Albert Ball had been awarded the VC, DSO and two Bars, MC and several foreign decorations, and had amassed 44 victories while serving with Nos 13, 11, 8, 60, 29 and 56 Squadrons. Ball is seen here in the cockpit of a No 56 Squadron S.E.5, a type he did not at first favour as he preferred the agility of the Nieuport sesquiplane fighters *(Bruce Robertson)*

France, bringing the first of the new Royal Aircraft Factory S.E.5 Scouts to the front. Powered like the Albatros with a water-cooled engine the S.E. was the first Allied scout to reach the front equipped with two guns – in this case a Vickers mounted in front of the pilot, synchronised to fire through the propeller arc, and a Lewis on the top wing. This latter weapon could be pulled down on its Foster mounting by the pilot, to be reloaded, to have a jam cleared, or to fire upwards into the belly of an aircraft above. This latter facility had been put to good use by several pilots of Nieuport Scouts, but notably by Capt Albert Ball, now one of No 56's flight commanders, and still at this time the RFC's top-scorer by a good margin.

At this time also, No 19 Squadron exchanged its almost useless F.E.12s for the first British SPAD S.VIIs and resumed fighting duties, while No 6 Squadron, which had been flying two-seater Nieuport 12s, replaced these

The popular single-seat Sopwith 'Pup' contributed greatly to the regaining of air supremacy by the Allies in 1916–17

**Though armed with only one 7.7 mm (0.303 in) synchronised machine gun and offering relatively modest performance in outright terms, the Sopwith Triplane packed its considerable wing area into three small wings for an excellent rate of climb and very good manoeuvrability. The impression it made on the Germans is attested by the number of triplanes that were then developed in Germany. This photograph was taken at Moscow airport during spring 1917** *(MARS)*

with Sopwith Pups. At Coudekerque on the coast, No 4 Naval Squadron replaced its 1½ Strutters with more Pups at this time, while No 6 Naval moved to La Bellevue to operate under RFC control, also operating two-gun aircraft – the latest Nieuport Scouts, fitted like the S.E.5 with both a Vickers and a Lewis.

The Arras battle opened on 9 April, and two days later Flight Sub Lieutenant J S T Fall impressively demonstrated the capabilities of the Pup in the hands of a competent pilot, claiming two Albatros and one Halberstadt scout shot down singlehanded in one engagement. Despite such isolated successes, the German Air Service now commenced to take its fearful toll on the RFC, and particularly on the reconnaissance and artillery spotting units. Rittmeister von Richthofen's *Jasta* 11 inflicted particular damage at this time, the unit commander achieving prominence. He claimed five victories on 28 April alone taking his personal total to over 50. One of his victims was Major H D Harvey-Kelly, commander of No 19 Squadron, who had been the first RFC pilot to land in France after war had been declared in August 1914. However, the Triplanes at least were beginning to come into their own, and two pilots, Roderick Dallas of No 1 Naval and Robert Little, were beginning long runs of success. By the end of the month von Richthofen was reporting that the Sopwith Triplane was the best Allied scout at the front, and was superior to the Albatros D.III and even the D.V, which was just about to be introduced.

On 1 May von Richthofen returned to Germany on leave, and almost as if this were a signal, the *Jastas'* activity slackened. Early during this month the RFC launched another all-out assault on the German kite balloons, whilst the Nieuport units also undertook a degree of ground attack work. Some of the Nieuport pilots were by now emulating Albert Ball and building up quite sizeable personal scores, notable amongst them being Jenkin, Campbell, Hazell and Fullard, all members of No 1 Squadron, all of whom would achieve totals of 20 or more. Another Nieuport pilot in No 60 Squadron, Captain W A Bishop, was also appearing frequently in

the RFC's communiqués, whilst No 56 Squadron was also beginning to make the presence of the S.E.5 felt when in the hands of pilots such as Rhys Davids, Hoidge, and G C Maxwell. The squadron's famous flight commander, Ball, was rapidly adding more victories to maintain his position at the top, but on 7 May, after a month at the front, he crashed to his death in unexplained circumstances; the award of a Victoria Cross was announced shortly after his loss.

During mid May No 10 Naval Squadron, another newly-formed Triplane unit, was also attached to the RFC. One of the flight commanders was a Canadian, Raymond Collishaw, who had already gained several victories and who during the next two months became probably the supreme exponent of the Sopwith Triplane. His all-Canadian 'Black Flight' claimed a record number of successes for the period, 30 of these accruing to Collishaw personally.

Considerable updating of RFC equipment took place during May, as existing units were re-equipped. No 11 Squadron received the latest F.2B version of the Bristol Fighter to replace its F.E.2bs, while No 24 and No 32 Squadrons exchanged their long-outdated D.H.2s for De Havilland's latest scout, the D.H.5. This aircraft featured an unusual back-stagger to its biplane wings, giving it a most distinctive appearance. It had already gained an unenviable, if somewhat undeserved reputation for being difficult to fly. Certainly its altitude performance did not compare favourably with that of the Pup, S.E.5 or SPAD, and it was armed only

The best two-seat fighter of World War 1 was the Bristol F.2B Fighter. It had originally been conceived for the reconnaissance role before being recast as a fighter. The type's first missions were little short of disastrous as its pilots opted to fly it as a conventional two-seater with the primary weapons capability resting with the operator of the trainable gun in the rear cockpit. Once experience had taught pilots to fly the Fighter as a single-seat fighter with emphasis on manoeuvring for offensive use of the fixed forward-firing gun, and the trainable gun behind the pilot now seen as an offensive/defensive bonus, the aircraft matured into an excellent fighter
*(Bruce Robertson)*

Seen here with Albert Ball in the cockpit and the Lewis gun carried on the upper-wing centre section pulled back to fire obliquely forward and upward in the fashion much favoured by Ball, this S.E.5 has the original type of semi-cockpit transparency that was disliked by virtually all pilots and soon removed in favour of a small windscreen
*(MARS)*

Canadian 'Billy' Bishop rose to the rank of Lieutenant Colonel. He is seen here in the cockpit of a Nieuport Nie.17 fighter while serving with No 60 Squadron early in 1917. The lone flyer was awarded the VC in June 1917 on the basis of his own uncorroborated claim of downing three Albatros Scouts in one mission *(Bruce Robertson)*

with one machine gun. It cannot be said to have been the happiest choice for these hard-pressed but experienced units.

No 23 Squadron had also got rid of their F.E.2bs, exchanging these for five SPAD S.VIIs which they took into action during the month. Notably, No 4 Naval Squadron at Dunkerque took delivery of the first of another of the war's truly classic fighters, the Sopwith Camel. Although tricky to fly and unforgiving to the novice, once mastered the Camel was quite incredibly manoeuvrable, and was soon to become famous for fighting its way out of trouble rather than flying away from it. Fitted with a rotary engine – a variety of different types of which were to power the aircraft during its relatively long service – and armed with two Vickers guns, representing the most effective armament to date on an Allied aircraft – this little machine soon became the most numerous scout in the RFC and RNAS, and was credited with shooting down more of its opponents than any other British type during the war.

On 7 June 1917 one of the more successful of the British offensives of the war commenced when a series of vast mines which had been planted beneath the German front line positions in secret tunnels dug by the engineers, were set off in the largest man-made series of explosions seen or heard up to that date. Thus started the Battle of Messines.

The month was also marked by the award of another Victoria Cross to an RFC scout pilot, 'Billy' Bishop of No 60 Squadron. The young Canadian ex-cavalry officer had returned from a lone dawn attack on a German airfield, during which he claimed to have shot down three hostile scouts which had taken off to try and intercept him.

By this time the S.E.5 had been developed into the improved S.E.5a, the first of these aircraft reaching No 56 Squadron during the month.

Seen in front of a Bristol Monoplane fighter, a type of which only a few were completed as a result of official antipathy to the monoplane layout, at Turnberry in Scotland during 1918 are (left to right with their final scores) Captains J Leacroft (22 victories), E D Atkinson (8), G J C Maxwell (26), Taylor and Le Gallais *(Bruce Robertson)*

However, on 13 June Gotha bombers had made a large-scale daylight attack on London, leading to a public outcry regarding the lack of adequate defence for the capital city. Consequently, Nos 56 and 66 Squadrons were immediately removed from the front, No 56 to the London area and No 66 to Calais, where its Pups were to intercept any further such attacks en route. No repeat attacks actually transpired during the next few weeks, and both units were soon released to return to the Western Front.

Yet another new British scout had been developed at this time. This was the Bristol M.1, a monoplane of good performance, which was approaching service readiness early in 1917. When the D.H.5 had proved to be disappointing, and No 56 Squadron was suffering various technical difficulties with its S.E.5s, it had been hoped that this aircraft might prove to be a viable alternative. Unfortunately, an inbred distrust of the monoplane configuration by the British authorities, occasioned by certain structural failures in earlier designs, led to delays, and production remained very limited, all available aircraft finally being despatched instead to the Middle East during June.

Several leading pilots continued to do well during June, most notably Raymond Collishaw, but just prior to his arrival at the front the most successful pilot during the preceding month had, rather oddly, been a member of No 20 Squadron, flying an F.E.2d. Captain F H Thayre and his gunner, Captain F B Cubbon, became the highest scoring of all F.E.2 crews, accounting for 20 enemy machines in this type – 15 of them during May 1917!

The first successes for the new Camels were achieved on 5 June when Flight Commander A M Shook of No 4 Naval Squadron claimed an Albatros D.V shot down and a two-seater out of control. During the month Nos 3 and 6 Naval Squadrons also re-equipped with this new scout, while Nos 8 and 9 Naval Squadrons also began replacing their existing machines with them. The RFC's No 70 Squadron also converted to Camels from 1¹/₂ Strutters, and by the end of July, No 45 Squadron also began to receive batches of the new aircraft. No 41 Squadron at last rid themselves of surviving single-seat 'pushers' when D.H.5s were received to replace their F.E.8s, and No 60 Squadron began converting from Nieuports to S.E.5s.

The Airco D.H.5 (right) was an indifferent fighter whose backward-staggered wing cellule was designed to offer the pilot exceptional fields of vision but also conferred some unpleasant handling characteristics including the tendency to stall at a comparatively high speed. The SPAD S.VII (left) was an altogether superior type used by the British only in small numbers. This example shows decided damage to the control surfaces including a crumpled upper part to the rudder, damage to the starboard upper aileron and a missing port upper aileron. Behind the S.VII, and identifiable by its serial number, is an Avro Type 504A (*Bruce Robertson*)

This DFW C V general-purpose biplane was brought down on 12 July 1917 by Lieutenants A P F Rhys Davids and K K Muspratt of No 56 Squadron, one of the most successful British fighter units of the war. Rhys Davids eventually achieved 25 'kills' and Muspratt claimed six *(Bruce Robertson)*

The Germans too were upgrading their equipment, the first Albatros D.Vs and D.VAs reaching the front during May, several *Jastas* having these new aircraft on strength during the summer. On 6 July, having returned to *Jasta* 11 after a long leave of absence from the front, Manfred von Richthofen was shot down in combat with an F.E.2d, and was wounded in the head, once again being off operations for some weeks as a result.

For the first time during July Allied scouts operated as fighter-bombers, carrying light Cooper bombs to drop on targets of opportunity. It was also during this month that Captain Arthur Coningham of No 32 Squadron became the most successful pilot to fly the D.H.5, claiming nine victories during a period of just two weeks mid month. July and August also saw the three great Naval aces claiming their last successes with the Triplane, this successful aircraft bowing out of front line service after an extremely brief career. Little's score had by now reached 37, 24 of them gained whilst flying the Triplane, while Dallas' total had now reached 20. Collishaw, Fall and Little were now closely following the RFC's 'Billy' Bishop towards passing Ball's total.

The British now continued their offensive in Flanders by launching the Battle of Ypres on 31 July, designed to advance along the Belgian coast as far as Ostende, capturing Bruges and Zeebrugge in order to deny these ports to the Germans, who were employing them as bases for their

This Rumpler C V general-purpose aircraft was shot down by Captain James McCudden on 21 October 1917 *(Bruce Robertson)*

This trio of No 56 Squadron pilots are, from left to right, Captain James McCudden, Captain G J C Maxwell and E L Zinc (*Bruce Robertson*)

U-Boats, which were creating great concern by their depredations in the Atlantic. During this particular battle much use was made for the first time of scouts in the ground attack role, co-ordinated with the infantry advance, and here the D.H.5s proved their particular suitability for this task, although the purpose of the new offensive was not to be achieved.

By this time, however, the variety and number of fighting scout units available on the Western Front for the RFC and RNAS had reached a record level. Nos 18 and 25 Squadrons had exchanged their F.E.2bs for D.H.4s during June, in doing so becoming bomber units, and No 27 Squadron was about to follow suit.

In England several additional squadrons of fighting scouts had been formed for home defence purposes against any further Gotha raids. The last such raid occured on 22 August, thereafter the German units changing their tactics to night raiding, as the daytime opposition was threatening to become too dangerous. As a consequence, whilst some of the new units began training in the night fighting role, most had become effectively surplus to requirements. They were Nos 33, 36, 37, 38, 39, 44, 61, 75, 76, 77, 78 and 112 Squadrons.

This Bristol M.1C Monoplane was one of five such aircraft which was test flown by Captain James McCudden (*Bruce Robertson*)

Awarded the DSO and MC, Captain Andrew Edward McKeever was a pilot who helped to ensure his success by personal involvement in the maintenance and harmonisation of his aeroplane, especially the engine and gun. He was the top-scorer on the Bristol Fighter, which he flew with No 11 Squadron during 1917 (*Bruce Robertson*)

The Germans also began to change their tactics on the Western Front at this time to challenge the growing number of Anglo-French fighting units. Chosen *Jagdstaffeln* were now grouped together to form *Jagdgeschwadern* when such concentration proved desirable or necessary to achieve air superiority over any particular part of the front – usually when offensive operations were taking place on the ground. On occasions, other *Jastas* would be more informally and temporarily grouped into *Jagdgruppen*.

The first of these new groupings created JG I, based at Courtrai under the command of Manfred von Richthofen. This encompassed von Richthofen's own *Jasta* 11 with *Jastas* 4, 6 and 10. During August this unit received the two pre-production test examples of a new Fokker triplane, produced as a consequence of the impact of the Sopwith Triplane on its opponents. One was employed by von Richthofen himself, who was not initially greatly impressed with it, although he did obtain his 60th victory whilst flying it. The other was handed to one of the *Jasta* commanders, Leutnant Werner Voss, who rapidly made good use of its exceptional manoeuvrability, claiming ten victories between 30 August and 23 September to raise his personal total to 48. During the latter date however, while engaged with an S.E.5 of No 60 Squadron, he was attacked by six S.E.5as of No 56 Squadron led by Capt James McCudden, and after a long fight the second highest-scoring German of the day succumbed to fire from Lieutenant Arthur Rhys Davids, who also shot down an Albatros which attempted to come to his aid.

No 56 Squadron was without doubt the RFC's premier unit at this time, and on 30 September claimed its 200th victory. Only No 20 Squadron with its F.E.2ds had previously achieved such a total. There was no leading British Empire ace active at the front at this time, however, for after having passed Ball's total during August, Bishop had gone home on leave to Canada to get married with his total at 47. Little, with a similar total, and Collishaw, were both also being rested at this time.

A new unit to arrive in France in September was No 68 Squadron, manned entirely by personnel of the Australian Flying Corps (AFC), and equipped with D.H.5s. During that month No 43 Squadron re-equipped with Camels, the unit's elderly 1½ Strutters having been suffering fairly heavy casualties recently. This marked the disappearance from the Western Front of these one-time stalwarts. Two further new units to arrive before the end of September were No 28 Squadron with Camels and No 84 Squadron with S.E.5as. They were followed in October by No 64 Squadron with yet more of the disappointing D.H.5s; already however, No 41 Squadron was gratefully exchanging its aircraft of this type for the S.E.5a – an aircraft which No 40 Squadron also started to take on strength to replace its faithful Nieuports.

The production version of the Fokker triplane, the Dr.I, began delivery to JG I in mid August, but within days two experienced pilots had been killed in crashes in these aircraft and the remainder were grounded, pending investigation. Another new German scout appearing at this time was the Pfalz D.III, a good-looking aircraft, similar in general appearance to the Albatros D.V; it proved to be rather less effective than the latter, although it was to equip quite a number of *Jastas*.

No 1 Naval Squadron's attachment to the RFC on the Western Front came to an end on 2 November, and the Triplanes departed without ever having engaged their new German counterpart in the air. The last Triplane victory was claimed on 1 November by Flight Lieutenant H V Rowley, and within a few weeks of withdrawing, No 1 Naval had also received Camels.

There was to be no let-up in the efforts to increase the RFC's strength and to improve its equipment. During early November No 46 Squadron exchanged its Pups for Camels, and yet more of these sturdy fighters reached France with Nos 3 and 65 Squadrons, the former previously a Corps reconnaissance unit.

On 20 November the Battle of Cambrai was launched, for the first time the British employing tanks in numbers in a surprise attack without an initial artillery bombardment. Supported by Camels of Nos 3 and 46 Squadrons, and by D.H.5s of Nos 64 and 68 (AFC) Squadrons, which attacked ground targets, the shock element allowed a quite deep penetration through the German lines to be achieved. Unfortunately, adequate reserves had not been provided to exploit such a success, and advantage was not taken of it. The spearheads were ultimately held and then driven back. For this operation, the RFC had amassed 134 scout aircraft in an area where initially they were faced by no more than 12 aircraft of a single *Jasta*. Three days after the attack started, JG I was moved to the area and very heavy fighting in the air then developed.

November saw the departure from the front of two of the RFC's leading pilots. Captain P F Fullard of No 1 Squadron, at the time the top-scorer still in action, broke his leg whilst playing football and was evacuated to England for a long spell of convalescence. Capt A E McKeever, a Canadian with No 11 Squadron, also departed on leave. With his observers he had claimed 31 victories with the Bristol F.2B Fighter, the highest total to be claimed by a pilot of these aircraft throughout the war.

A famous photograph of Nieuport Type 24bis and 27 single-seat Scouts of No 1 Squadron lined up in the snow at Bailleul in December 1917. The aircraft in the foreground was initially flown by Captain W W Rogers (9 victories) before being passed on to Captain G B Moore (10 victories) who is seen in the picture

This Nieuport Nie.27 was operated by No 1 Squadron, which at the time depicted in December 1917 was based at Bailleul. Among the high-scoring aces who passed through this squadron were Captain P F Fullard (40 victories), Major T F Hazell (43), Captain F R McCall (35), Captain R T C Hoidge (29), Captain W C Campbell (23), Captain P J Clayson (29) and Captain W L Harrison (22) *(Bruce Robertson)*

In Italy meanwhile, after a long quiet spell the Austro-Hungarian forces had launched a major offensive at Caporetto which broke through and put the Italian Army into flight. British and French expeditionary forces were at once despatched to aid their ally in Northern Italy, the British contingent being accompanied by three squadrons of Camels which began departing France from November onwards. No 28 Squadron, only recently arrived at the front, was the first to go, followed by No 66 Squadron (now converted to the new aircraft from Pups) and No 45 Squadron – one of the most experienced units available. These squadrons served on this new front throughout most of the coming year. Initially they met both German and Austro-Hungarian aircraft, but after March 1918 solely the latter opposed them with Offag-built Albatros D.IIIs, Aviatiks, Berg D.Is and Phoenix Scouts, together with several types of two-seaters, mainly of Brandenburg manufacture.

With the arrival of winter and an end to the campaigning season on the Western Front, the D.H.5s were further phased out, Nos 24, 32, 64 and 68(AFC) Squadrons all ridding themselves of these aircraft in favour of S.E.5as during December and January, while No 54 Squadron bade farewell to the last of the Pups in front line service, these being replaced by Camels. With growing quantities of modern fighting scouts now at last available, a few S.E.5as were also sent to the Middle East for use by Nos 17 and 47 Squadrons in Macedonia and No 111 Squadron in Egypt. These units also received a few of the Bristol M.1C monoplane, which proved to be highly thought of by all who flew it, many considering it to be the best fighting aircraft to be supplied to them during 1918.

In the later stages of 1917 No 19 Squadron had supplemented and then replaced its rapidly-ageing SPAD S.VIIs with the more powerful S.XIII, which was also armed with two guns. In December No 23 Squadron fully re-equipped with these aircraft which they put to good use. During January 1918, however, No 19 Squadron exchanged its SPADs for a new aircraft, the Sopwith Dolphin. This aircraft featured back-stagger biplane wings, not unlike those of the D.H.5, and for this reason there was a degree of initial prejudice against the aircraft. This proved to be ill-founded, for the Dolphin rapidly proved to be an excellent aircraft with an outstanding high altitude performance. Unlike previous Sopwith scouts, it was powered by a water-cooled engine, which initially caused some reliability

The Sopwith 5F Dolphin showing the troublesome 'crossbar' mounted, upward-firing Lewis guns

problems, although these were subsequently solved satisfactorily. It featured an unusually powerful armament, with two fixed Vickers guns above the engine and two flexible Lewis guns affixed to the top wing. In service the latter soon tended to be removed as superfluous. Later in the war arrangements were incorporated for a pair of Lewis guns to be fixed on the top of the lower wing, firing forward outside the propeller arc; as these could not be rearmed in flight, the increased weight was considered to outweigh the advantage offered, and few pilots favoured them.

During 1917 there had been increasing aerial activity along the area of the Channel coast. Initially seaplane elements of the German Navy had faced their opposite numbers in the RNAS's St Pol Defence Flight. These forces had been supplemented steadily with growing numbers of fighting scouts, the RNAS Flight receiving Sopwith Pups to provide support and defence for the units of the British Grand Fleet. During September the Pups had given way to Camels, and by the end of the year the Flight was at full squadron strength, becoming No 13 Naval Squadron, commanded by Squadron Commander Raymond Collishaw, recently returned from Canada.

A naval pilot who ranked third on the list of British and Empire aces of World War 1, Raymond Collishaw (left) was of Canadian birth and became an officer of the Royal Air Force when it was created by the amalgamation of the RNAS and Royal Flying Corps on 1 April 1918. He is seen here in conversation with Captain A T Whealey, a five-victory ace. Raymond Collishaw in 1919 added two Soviet aeroplanes to his tally of 60 'kills' in World War 1 *(Bruce Robertson)*

# 1918: THE ROYAL AIR FORCE IS BORN

**E**arly 1918 saw the arrival in France of several more new units. Nos 71 and 80 Squadrons were equipped with Camels, whilst No 79 Squadron brought more of the new Dolphins. Nos 67 and 68 Squadrons (the former based in Egypt) were all-Australian units, as was No 71 Squadron, and shortly after the arrival of these new units, these three were renumbered as Nos 1, 2 and 4 Squadrons, Australian Flying Corps.

On 16 February 1918 Captain James McCudden of No 56 Squadron claimed three victories to become the first Empire pilot to exceed a total of 50. However, this had occurred at a moment of great danger for the Allies. The French Army had been seriously weakened by the vast losses suffered at Verdun, and was troubled by a number of resulting mutinies. The British had also suffered grievously during the offensives of 1917, and this had been exacerbated by the need to despatch troops to Italy. Due to the problems faced by the French, a further 28 miles of the front had also been passed over to the British. Troops from the USA, which had entered the war during 1917, were expected, but none had yet arrived.

The Germans on the other hand had achieved an armistice with Imperial Russia after inflicting some devastating defeats on that nation, and consequently were able to relocate substantial additional forces to the West. Before America's abundant manpower could arrive to swing the balance, the Germans knew that they must strike now if the war was ever to be won.

Preparations had, therefore, rapidly proceeded for a huge offensive against the British 3rd and 5th Army fronts to the north and south of Arras. Many *Feldfliegerabteilungen* – the Corps reconnaissance aircraft of the German Air Service – had been converted to the *Schlacht* (fighter-bomber) role, providing close ground attack support to the infantry. The number of *Jastas* had been increased to 80, though many were equipped with obsolescent types and were under strength. Units from other areas of the front were concentrated in the critical area, allowing 326 fighting scouts to be made available. Although together the French and British could muster a much larger quantity of such aircraft, actually facing the assault forces the British had only 261 scout aircraft immediately available .

At this point RFC scout squadrons had been reorganised to give them an establishment of 24 aircraft, together with sufficient administrative support to allow unit commanders to fly regularly with their pilots if they so desired. In the past their duties had resulted in most remaining

**Before his death in a flying accident on 9 July 1918, Major James Thomas Byford McCudden had been awarded the VC, DSO and Bar, MC and Bar, MM and Croix de Guerre, and had gained 57 aerial victories. This total puts him fourth on the list of British aces** (*Bruce Robertson*)

In February 1918 Captain James McCudden of No 56 Squadron fitted the four-blade propeller of his S.E.5a with the spinner from an LVG C V two-seater that he had shot down on 30 November 1917 *(Bruce Robertson)*

desk-bound, leaving the task of leadership in the air to the flight commanders. This had never been so on the other side of the lines, and here, despite some two years of almost constant action, Manfred von Richthofen was still leading JG I in the air – an inspiration to all German scout pilots. On 12 March his pilots shot down four out of nine Bristol Fighters of newly-arrived No 62 Squadron. Next day this unit responded when one of its crews assisted in shooting down Lothar von Richthofen, who was badly wounded.

The great German offensive of spring 1918 opened on 21 March, supported by large formations of *Schlacht* aircraft. All available British units were thrown into the battle, most making many attacks against the advancing enemy on the ground. Reinforcements were rushed to the area and fighting accelerated as the opposing scouts battled for control of the skies to assist progress on the ground.

At this moment, No 29 Squadron, still flying its Nieuport Scouts – the last RFC unit still to be doing so – claimed the last successes for these elderly fighters on 23rd, then withdrew to replace them with S.E.5as as swiftly as possible. Next day Captain John Trollope of No 43 Squadron claimed six victories between dawn and dusk in his Camel.

The greatest crisis occurred on 25th, when the British Army received its famous 'backs-to-the-wall' order as it was forced to withdraw. Some squadrons experienced shelling of their airfields, although evacuation of

Named 'The White Feather' and painted white, this is the Sopwith Camel flown by Captain A H Cobby, the 29-victory Australian ace of No 4 Squadron, Australian Flying Corps, when he was an instructor *(Bruce Robertson)*

Seen here with a two-seat training conversion of the Sopwith Camel single-seat fighter, Captain William Gordon Claxton was a Canadian pilot who claimed 37 victories in a period of only three months while serving with No 41 Squadron. Awarded the DSO and DFC and Bar, Claxton was brought down behind the German lines on 17 August 1918 after being wounded in the head, but survived to become a successful financial journalist
*(Bruce Robertson)*

These personnel of No 85 Squadron were captured by the camera at St Omer in northern France on 21st June 1918. Their mount was the S.E.5a. Two notable figures in the pilot line-up are two Americans, Lieutenants Lawrence K Calahan and Elliott White Springs (sixth and seventh from left). Calahan was later transferred to the American 148th Aero Squadron and ended the war with five victories, while Springs achieved four victories with No 85 Squadron before being transferred to the 148th Aero Squadron, with which he claimed another eight victories
*(Bruce Robertson)*

the most forward units had commenced as early as the 22nd. Not surprisingly, with the extent of the aerial fighting now occurring, many new Empire aces appeared at this time. A few became well-known names, but most remained in almost total obscurity. From March until the end of the war many pilots claimed more than 20 victories, but most received very little publicity – certainly much less than had the most successful pilots of 1917. Men such as Beauchamp Proctor, MacLaren, McElroy, Carter, and many others were in the thick of the fighting at this time.

The Royal Air Force was born on 1 April 1918, barely noticed in the heat of battle. On that date the RFC and RNAS merged to form a single, independent third service. Initially Army ranks were retained, the Naval personnel all having their existing RNAS ranks appropriately converted, whilst their squadrons had the number 200 added, so that for instance No 1 Naval Squadron became No 201 Squadron, and so on. Subsequently a complete new RAF rank structure replaced the Army ranks, but this did not occur until after the war. For the time being Naval Flight Sub Lieutenants and Flight Lieutenants became 2nd Lieutenants and Lieutenants respectively, Flight Commanders became Captains, Squadron Commanders became Majors, and Wing Commanders became Lieutenant Colonels.

Seen here in the cockpit of a captured Fokker D.VII, Germany's best fighter of World War 1, is Captain Andrew Edward McKeever, a Canadian pilot of No 11 Squadron. McKeever was the most successful exponent of the Bristol F.2B Fighter, a two-seat machine in which his gunner was Sergeant (later Lieutenant) L F Powell. McKeever survived the war only to die as a result of a car accident in 1919, and his victory tally of 31 German aircraft included eight by Powell, making the gunner an ace in his own right *(Bruce Robertson)*

A Canadian, Major William George Barker flew with Nos 9, 4, 15, 28, 139 and 201 Squadrons in a fighting career that witnessed 53 victories and the receipt of the VC, DSO, MC and two Bars, and four foreign decorations. Barker won the VC for an epic fight late in the war when he encountered up to 60 Fokker D.VII fighters in four groups, and shot down four of them before crash-landing in the British lines with three wounds *(Bruce Robertson)*

At the time this change occurred, the air forces could be said to be having a relatively decisive effect on events on the ground for the first time. Although initially outnumbered, the British squadrons were attacking the advancing troops, their supply columns and bases sufficiently to have a disruptive effect which played a significant part in preventing a complete German breakthrough.

The Germans attacked again on 9 April, this time on a hitherto quiet front in the Lys area, largely manned by inexperienced Portuguese troops, who broke under the pressure. Again the new RAF's units were thrown in to help save the day as the enemy achieved their breakthrough. On the 12th Captain Henry Woollett of No 43 Squadron claimed six victories, repeating the recent similar success of John Trollope of the same unit only a few days earlier.

Another notable event occurred on 21 April when Rittmeister Manfred von Richthofen, still the top-scoring fighter pilot of the war with 80 victories to his credit, was shot down and killed. He was engaged with Camels of No 209 Squadron (the old No 9 Naval) when he fell, and his demise was initially credited to Captain A R Brown of that unit, although subsequent research has shown fairly certainly that he was actually killed by a bullet from an Australian-manned machine gun on the ground.

In the midst of the fighting more new units continued to arrive. April brought No 74 Squadron with S.E.5as, No 87 Squadron with Dolphins and No 88 Squadron with Bristol Fighters, while No 85 Squadron with S.E.5as followed in May. At this time too, No 23 Squadron exchanged their SPAD S.XIIIs for Dolphins, thereby standardising RAF scout equipment in France on four types – the S.E.5a, Camel, Dolphin and Bristol F.2B.

Two new German scouts were also appearing at this time. The more numerous was the Fokker D.VII (frequently referred to by RAF pilots simply as the Fokker Biplane), whilst the excellent Siemens-Schuckert D.III was only met in much smaller numbers. The D.VII rapidly became the Allies' main opponent during the remaining months of the war; the initial version was powered by a Mercedes engine, although a later – and more dangerous – version featured a BMW powerplant. British scouts

Major William Barker's Sopwith Camel fighter of No 139 Squadron is captured by the camera during a fast climb from an Italian airfield (MARS)

were also to be up-engined during this period, the performance of the Camel particularly being enhanced when the Gnome-Rhône or Clerget rotary engines were replaced by a Bentley-manufactured unit of greater power.

During this period the final German push was launched on 27 May, but within three days their advance was held on the River Marne, and the last great offensive against the Allies on the Western Front had come to an end.

## OTHER FRONTS

On the Italian Front a new unit, known initially as Z Flight, had been formed early in March 1918, equipped with Bristol Fighters, and administered by No 34 Squadron, an R.E.8-equipped Corps reconnaissance unit; this flight was now expanded to form No 139 Squadron. Initially it was commanded by Major W G Barker, who had previously flown with both No 28 and No 66 Squadrons; Barker took his Camel with him to his new command, which he continued to fly. He had rapidly emerged as by far the most successful scout pilot of the expeditionary force in this area. Several others were doing well, however, notably Captain M B Frew of No 45 Squadron.

On 30 March Lieutenant A Jerrard and two other pilots of No 66 Squadron were engaged in a fight with a reported 19 Austro-Hungarian aircraft; Jerrard was shot down and became a prisoner, but his two companions returned to report that he had shot down three of their

Extreme conditions put a severe test on aeroplanes used in the Palestine campaign. Here, two B.E.2cs moored in the open are about to be overwhelmed by a 'dust devil'

A pilot of No 85 Squadron poses in front of his S.E.5a fighter with the unit's proud 'scoreboard' for 21 June 1918 *(Bruce Robertson)*

Photographed early in his career, William 'Billy' Bishop was reputedly an excellent pilot and a superb marksman *(Bruce Robertson)*

opponents before falling himself, and consequently he was awarded a Victoria Cross. In fact there appears to have been little or no foundation for the claims made on his behalf.

The Austro-Hungarians launched their own major offensive during June, but this too was held. The third major member of the Central Powers alliance (Turkey) was also in difficulty throughout the Middle East, where Allied forces were steadily increasing the pressure. No 72 Squadron had recently arrived at Basra in Mesopotamia (now Iraq), equipped with a variety of scout types, while No 150 Squadron had formed in Macedonia from the fighting flights of Nos 17 and 47 Squadrons, equipped with S.E.5as, Bristol M.1Cs, Nieuports, and subsequently some Camels. In Palestine the all-Australian No 67 Squadron, which had become No 1 AFC Squadron, had replaced a mixed bag of B.E.12s, Martinsyde G.l00s and other types with Bristol F.2B Fighters. More of these aircraft had also been provided to No 111 Squadron, operating alongside Nieuports, which were themselves then replaced by S.E.5as.

## SUMMER 1918

Amongst the newly-arrived units, No 85 Squadron was led by Major 'Billy' Bishop, VC, who rapidly set about regaining his position as the Empire's top-scorer. By mid June, adopting his preferred lone hunting tactics, he had claimed a further 25 victories in less than a month to reach a total of 72. At that stage he was removed from the front at the request of the Canadian Government, returning to England to assist in the formation of the new Canadian Air Force.

During June 1918 the first specialised night fighter squadron had reached France, although as mentioned, such units had been operating over England against Gotha bombers for some months. No 151 Squadron, equipped with specially modified Camels, arrived to combat German night raids on Allied supply dumps and airfields, which were becoming increasingly effective.

July saw the arrival of one of the last two RAF scout units to reach the front before hostilities ceased. This was No 92 Squadron, equipped with S.E.5as and commanded by Major Arthur Coningham, the ex-D.H.5 exponent. Meanwhile Bishop's place at the head of No 85 Squadron had been taken by Major E 'Mick' Mannock, previously a flight commander with No 74 Squadron, who was rapidly building up a substantial personal tally. On 26 July however, Mannock was shot down in flames after successfully attacking a two-seater, and was killed. Following the end of the war a reassessment of his achievements led to a posthumous award of the Victoria Cross.

Highly-regarded within the service as a tactician and patrol leader, Mannock had been virtually unknown to the public up to this point. The citation to his VC credited him with 59 victories, but subsequently his

Seen in the cockpit of an S.E.5a fighter with no Lewis gun on the Foster quadrant mounting over the upper-wing centre section, this is Edward 'Mick' Mannock, with 61 victories the highest-scoring British ace of World War 1 *(Bruce Robertson)*

first biographer, another notable ace of No 74 Squadron, Capt J I T 'Taffy' Jones, claimed that Mannock had gained 73 victories, putting him ahead of Bishop. It is known that Jones did not have a high regard for the latter, whilst clearly he idolised Mannock. The Air Ministry never officially denied Jones' claim, and this total came to be accepted over the years. However many years of detailed research has indicated that it is extremely unlikely that Mannock ever claimed 73 successes.

## ——— ENTER THE AMERICANS ———

On the Western Front the RAF had been further reinforced by two squadrons of United States Air Service personnel equipped with Clerget-engined Camels. These units, the 17th and 148th Aero Squadrons operated as part of the RAF's 65th Wing until the last few weeks of the war.

It was now the turn of the Allies, at last being reinforced by fresh American divisions, to launch what rapidly became the last great offensive against the Germans on the Western Front. Launched on 8 August 1918, this attack was fully supported by both tanks and aircraft, employed effectively and in co-operation with the infantry. The Battle of Baupaume on 21 August was followed by the Battle of the Scarpe on 26th, whilst on 28th the last great attack on the Somme commenced.

HM King George V inspects squadron commanders in northern France on 8 August 1918, the date on which the great British offensive at Amiens marked the 'black day of the German army' and signalled the imminent Allied victory in World War 1. Evident behind the king, in a naval cap, is Raymond Collishaw *(Bruce Robertson)*

Photographed at Izel-les-Hameau on 8 July 1918, this line-up of the pilots and Sopwith Camel fighters of No 203 Squadron includes, nearest the camera, the machine flown by Lieutenant Colonel Raymond Collishaw when he shot down Fokker D.VII fighters on 15 and 29 August and 26 September of that year *(Bruce Robertson)*

In the air the Sopwith Camel was becoming outclassed by the new BMW-engined Fokker D.VIIs with which most of the leading German scout units were now re-equipped. Although still able to give a good account of itself in the hands of experienced pilots – particularly in its Bentley-engined form – losses began to rise alarmingly amongst less-experienced pilots. On 26 August the US 17th Aero Squadron engaged D.VIIs of JG III, losing six of their 11 Camels, whilst on 5 September No 4 AFC Squadron, a unit which had suffered but few losses so far, lost four out of five Camels in an engagement with the same German unit, claiming only a single 'out of control' victory in return. During the month, however, this Australian unit became one of the first to receive the new Sopwith Snipe fighter, which went a long way to restoring the balance.

At this time RAF scout squadrons had commenced operating in pairs on most occasions, a Camel unit at lower altitude, covered by an S.E.5a or Dolphin unit above. Sometimes all three types co-operated, when the splendid high altitude performance of the latter allowed them to fly at upwards of 18,000 feet. During August and September the Dolphin units were producing some very good results, pilots like R B Bannerman and the American F W Gillet of No 79 Squadron, and A W Vigers and A A N Pentland of No 87 Squadron claiming quite substantial numbers of successes.

It should be emphasised that, while the German Army was facing defeat on the ground, the Air Service was by no means in a similar state; although a reduction in training standards caused by a critical shortage of fuel led to heavy losses among inexperienced pilots, the *Jagdgeschwadern* and their *Jastas* remained formidable opponents to the very last day of the war. Indeed, the losses which they were able to inflict on the ever-growing quantities of Allied aircraft which were appearing – particularly against the generally inexperienced US units – were the highest of the whole war by a wide margin. On 31 October for instance the RAF alone lost 41 scouts in action, although claiming 67 German aircraft in return.

Nevertheless, by mid-September all the ground lost during the German Spring offensive had been regained. On 27th the Hindenburg Line, recognised as representing Germany's last real hope, was assaulted and overcome with remarkable rapidity, being fully in Allied hands by 8 October. An attack in the Lys area on 14 October achieved similar success, and three days later a Camel of No 210 Squadron was able to land at the Belgian port of Ostende, from which the Germans had just withdrawn.

On 27 October Major Barker, the great ace of the Italian Front, was involved in his last engagement, this time in France. Having returned from Italy to command an air fighting school in England, he sought a brief spell in France to update himself on conditions there. He was attached to No 201 Squadron, bringing with him a new Snipe. On a lone patrol on this particular date, having engaged and shot down a two-seater, he became involved in combat with a number of German aircraft from a unit which to this day remains unidentified. Reportedly he brought down three of the attacking D.VIIs before he was himself shot down, wounded in three places. He survived to be awarded a Victoria Cross.

Following Barker's award, only one further scout pilot was honoured with an award of the VC, Captain A W Beauchamp Proctor of No 84 Squadron, who had become the RAF's top 'balloon-buster' of the war, receiving such an award for his sustained record of success.

The Snipe was just making its presence felt when the war ended on 11 November 1918, growing numbers arriving in France, where No 4 AFC Squadron had joined No 43 Squadron in introducing them to action during October. No 208 Squadron began conversion, but too late to see action with the new aircraft. Captain E R King of No 4 AFC claimed seven victories in the new aircraft between 28 October and 4 November, to bring his total for the war to 26. Even the Snipe suffered an early reverse however, for on 4 November No 4 AFC Squadron lost five, three of them in one combat; two of these fell to Karl Bolle, one of the greatest of the German aces.

During this period, No 45 Squadron moved back to France from Italy to join the Independent Air Force in order to provide that force's strategic

Basically a development of the Camel to take advantage of the 171.5 kW (230 hp) Bentley BR.2 rotary engine, the Sopwith Snipe entered service only in the last months of World War 1. Only 200 such aircraft had been completed by the Armistice of November 1918, but the Snipe became the fighter mainstay of the Royal Air Force into the early 1920s *(Bruce Robertson)*

bombers with a degree of fighter escort over German territory, where losses had been rising. Whilst awaiting re-equipment with a long-range version of the Snipe, the unit briefly resumed operations with Camels.

In Italy, late in October, the Allies achieved a great victory against the Austro-Hungarians at Vittorio Veneto. The collapse of the enemy here led to the general collapse of the whole Hapsburg Empire in central Europe. The Turkish Army had also been defeated in the Middle East by this time, while Germany was facing starvation and revolution at home. Consequently an Armistice was signed and came into effect at 11.00 hours on 11 November 1918. The war had ended.

## 1918–20

Following the conclusion of the war with Germany, elements of the RAF were despatched to North and South Russia to aid the White Russian forces fighting with the Bolsheviks, who had seized power during 1917. In the South General Denikin's forces were aided by No 47 Squadron, commanded by Major Raymond Collishaw. This unit, which operated on a mobile basis from a headquarters railway train, included a flight of Camels. These saw a degree of aerial combat against Red aircraft, Collishaw personally claiming two more victories here. While a number of pilots who had become aces during the Great War served here on one or other of the fronts, the one who is believed to have been the most successful was Captain S M Kinkead, although records of the operation here are sparse in the extreme.

Flight Lieutenant Ira Jones volunteered for service with the British expeditionary force sent to north Russia in 1919, and is here seen (at midnight in the long northern summer!) in the gunner's cockpit of an Airco D.H.9A bomber flown by Flying Officer Guy Carter (*Bruce Robertson*)

# THE NATURE OF CLAIMS

The basis upon which claims were made and totals assessed during the birth of aerial fighting differed from nation to nation, and frequently differed also from the various bases adopted during World War 2, which have subsequently become familiar to those interested in the subject. For the British Empire air forces in the Great War, the basis also differed to an extent from year to year as the situation at the front changed.

The Germans from the start applied a strict set of rules, which was adhered to throughout the whole war, with some possible relaxation during the final weeks of fighting. In order to be credited with a victory, a German pilot either had to have independent confirmation, for instance from observers on the ground who actually saw the opponent crash, or alternatively by the recovery of the wreckage.

A little known naval pilot, Flight Commander R J O Compston of the Royal Naval Air Service's No 8 Squadron became Major Compston of the Royal Air Force's No 40 Squadron, and gained 25 aerial victories as well as the DSO, DSC and two Bars, and DFC *(Bruce Robertson)*

With the prevailing wind blowing from the west, and from the offensive tactics employed by the British units from early in the war, most fighting took place over, or within, the German lines. Consequently, compliance with these rules proved relatively easy. Where more than one pilot participated in a victory, no part shares were allocated; either the victory was credited to the pilot who had played the predominant role in the engagement (usually the senior man), or no individual credit was given, and the victory was credited to the unit as a whole.

The French generally required a similar degree of confirmation to that of the Germans. Claims made over enemy territory which could not be independently confirmed were generally credited only as 'probable' victories, and pilots' scores were frequently listed as so many confirmed plus so many probables.

Unlike the Germans, however, victories shared by two or more pilots were credited to the totals of each pilot, so that the cumulative total of the apparent scores of all the pilots in an *escadrille* usually amounted to a far higher figure than the number of actual victories claimed by the unit as a whole. This basis was applied in a similar form by other Allied nations, notably by the Italians and Belgians, and also by the US forces when operating with the French.

An officer who served with Nos 29, 56 and 41 Squadrons, Major Geoffrey Hilton Bowman gained 32 aerial victories in World War 1, together with a DSO, MC and Bar, and DFC *(Bruce Robertson)*

New Zealander K R Caldwell served with Nos 8, 60 and 74 Squadrons, scoring a total of 25 victories, reaching the rank of Major and winning the MC and DFC *(Bruce Robertson)*

When the initial engagements took place during 1915, however, because at the time it was a very difficult matter to shoot down another aircraft, victories credited in those early days to the British – and to a certain extent, to the French – air forces were frequently more of a moral than an actual nature. Hence an enemy aircraft which had been forced to land within its own territory, or one which had been 'driven down' to low level and obliged to retreat without completing its assigned duty, was considered to be a victory.

Such claims ceased to be listed after aerial fighting became more established during 1916, but for the British Empire units – and indeed, for those USAS units flying with them during 1918 – two main types of claim remained. The first category was 'destroyed' – either crashed or in flames – 'kills' which spoke for themselves. Although supposed to be independently confirmed by eye witnesses, the extent to which actions took place often deep

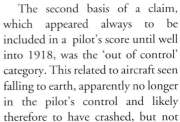

within German-held territory made claiming fraught with opportunities for error, and the benefit of the doubt frequently appears to have been exercised.

The second basis of a claim, which appeared always to be included in a pilot's score until well into 1918, was the 'out of control' category. This related to aircraft seen falling to earth, apparently no longer in the pilot's control and likely therefore to have crashed, but not seen so to do. In World War 2 parlance such claims would have been treated at best as 'probables' and on very many occasions must have been no more than the evasive action taken by opposing pilots after being attacked. Although World War 1 squadron diaries continued to list such claims and allocate them to pilots until the end of the war, by the summer of 1918 they were rarely being included in decoration citations any more.

Other claims included on quite frequent occasions included aircraft which had been forced to land in Allied territory and captured, which were clearly and quite convincingly, legitimate victories.

Tethered observation kite balloons were also included. These were dangerous targets to attack due to the degree of anti-aircraft support generally afforded to them. Since on the majority of occasions when shot down, they burst into flames in full view of the opposing trenches, confirmation was generally reliable. They were however, relatively immobile targets, and might fairly be considered to fall into a different category than aircraft. However, all combatant nations included them within pilots' scores.

As with the French and other Allies, the British treated shared successes as adding one complete victory to the total of each pilot taking part in the action. Because in 1916 and 1917 RFC units were suffering heavy casualties at a time when both the German and French media and propaganda services were making much of their fighting scout aces, the desire to show that the RFC too had such pilots may

Caught by the photographer while still under training, Edward 'Mick' Mannock had an astigmatic left eye, a condition that should have precluded any chance of a flying career. In fact Mannock became the highest scoring British ace of World War 1 with 61 victories *(Bruce Robertson)*

perhaps have allowed a quite wide and generous assessment of scores to be adopted. Certainly this may well have been one of the reasons why, despite the frequent use of individual scores in decoration citations etc, the British authorities were so adamant in their refusal to prepare official lists of successful pilots, or apparently to give any credence or authority to the matter.

Adopting the methodology described, it is possible to identify approaching 850 pilots who can be credited with five or more victories whilst flying scout aircraft, together with perhaps another 20 who were bomber or Corps aircraft pilots.

These matters need to be kept in mind when seeking to assess who were the most successful British Empire fighting scout pilots of the First World War, and in comparing their achievements with those of the pilots of the other warring nations.

These three aces all served with No 56 Squadron. From left to right are Captain James T B McCudden (57 victories), Captain Ian H D Henderson (5) and Captain G J C Maxwell (26) *(Bruce Robertson)*

# COLOUR PLATES

Author's note: This 12-page colour section profiles many of the aircraft flown by British and Empire aces of World War 1. Profile artists Mark Rolfe and Harry Dempsey have gone to great pains to illustrate the aircraft as accurately as possible within the limits of currently available sources. In certain cases where information is scarce, the profiles shown may be indicative only. No guarantee is given that the colours and other details are in all cases 100% accurate.

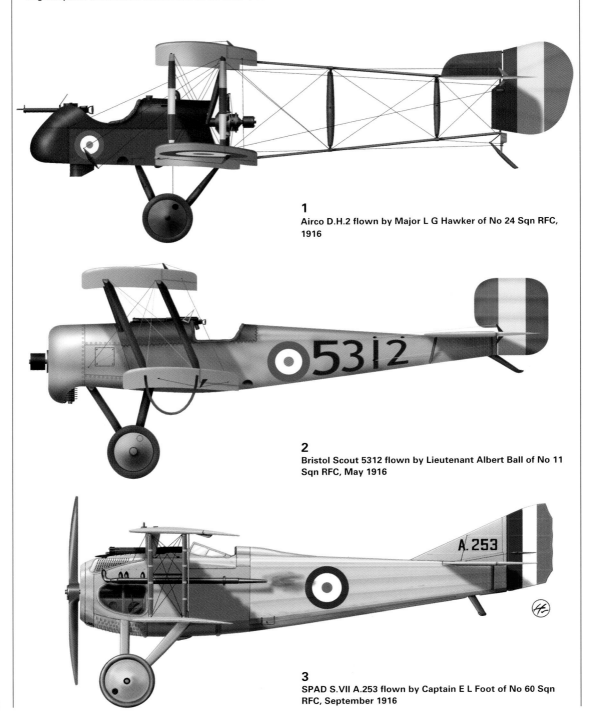

**1**
Airco D.H.2 flown by Major L G Hawker of No 24 Sqn RFC, 1916

**2**
Bristol Scout 5312 flown by Lieutenant Albert Ball of No 11 Sqn RFC, May 1916

**3**
SPAD S.VII A.253 flown by Captain E L Foot of No 60 Sqn RFC, September 1916

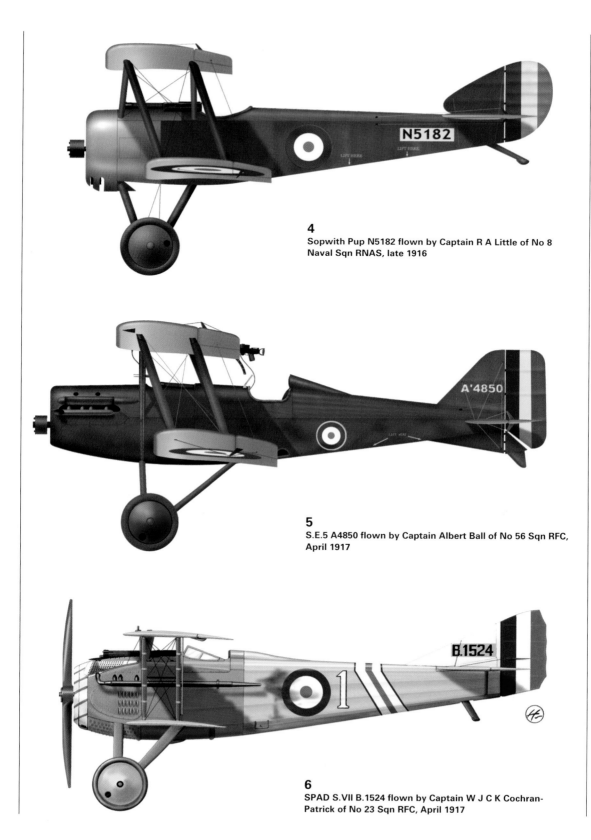

**4**
Sopwith Pup N5182 flown by Captain R A Little of No 8
Naval Sqn RNAS, late 1916

**5**
S.E.5 A4850 flown by Captain Albert Ball of No 56 Sqn RFC,
April 1917

**6**
SPAD S.VII B.1524 flown by Captain W J C K Cochran-
Patrick of No 23 Sqn RFC, April 1917

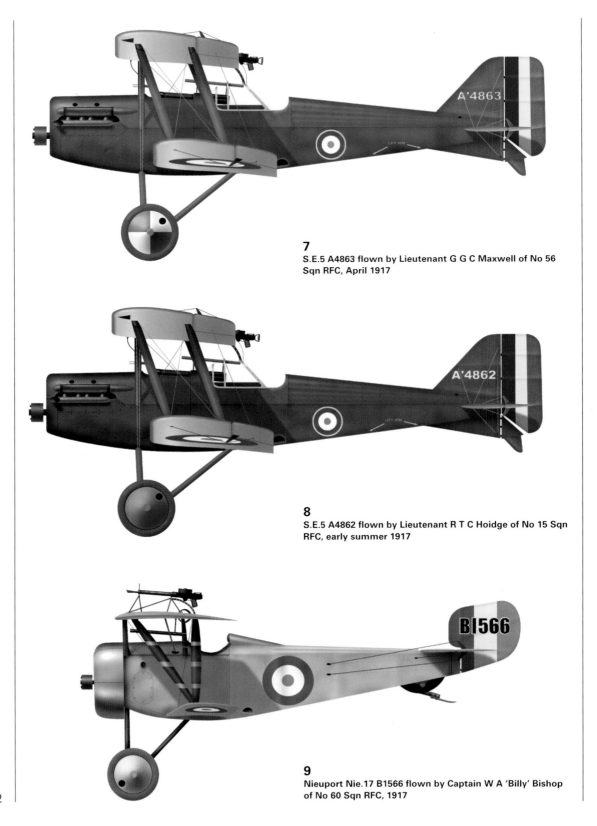

**7**
S.E.5 A4863 flown by Lieutenant G G C Maxwell of No 56
Sqn RFC, April 1917

**8**
S.E.5 A4862 flown by Lieutenant R T C Hoidge of No 15 Sqn
RFC, early summer 1917

**9**
Nieuport Nie.17 B1566 flown by Captain W A 'Billy' Bishop
of No 60 Sqn RFC, 1917

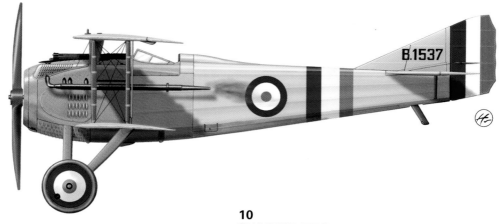

**10**
SPAD S.VII B.1537 flown by Lieutenant J M Child of No 19
Sqn RFC, May 1917

**11**
S.E.5 A4868 flown by Lieutenant A P F Rhys Davids of No 56
Sqn RFC, May 1917

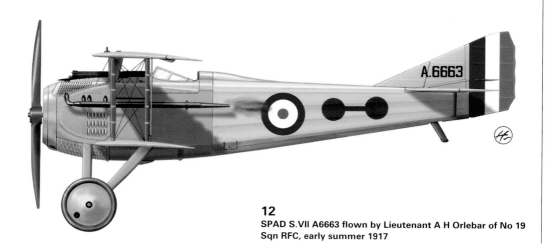

**12**
SPAD S.VII A6663 flown by Lieutenant A H Orlebar of No 19
Sqn RFC, early summer 1917

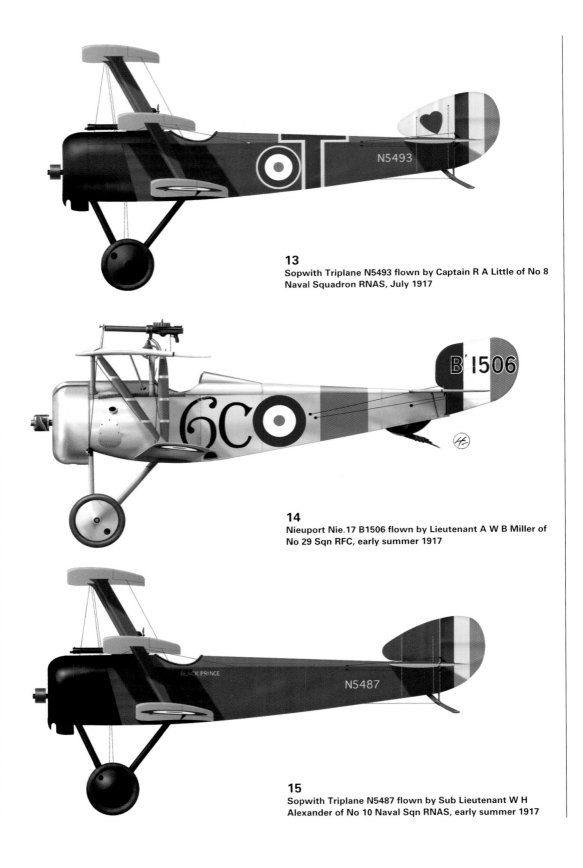

**13**
Sopwith Triplane N5493 flown by Captain R A Little of No 8
Naval Squadron RNAS, July 1917

**14**
Nieuport Nie.17 B1506 flown by Lieutenant A W B Miller of
No 29 Sqn RFC, early summer 1917

**15**
Sopwith Triplane N5487 flown by Sub Lieutenant W H
Alexander of No 10 Naval Sqn RNAS, early summer 1917

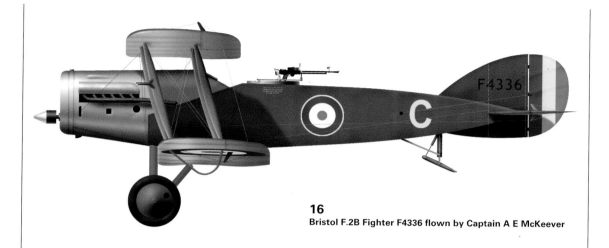

**16**
Bristol F.2B Fighter F4336 flown by Captain A E McKeever

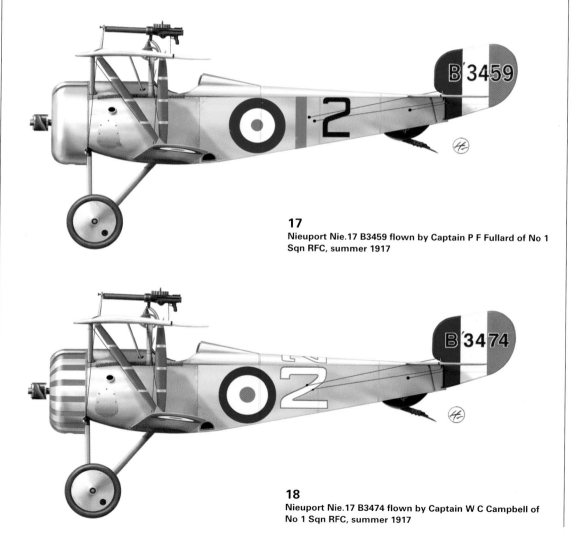

**17**
Nieuport Nie.17 B3459 flown by Captain P F Fullard of No 1
Sqn RFC, summer 1917

**18**
Nieuport Nie.17 B3474 flown by Captain W C Campbell of
No 1 Sqn RFC, summer 1917

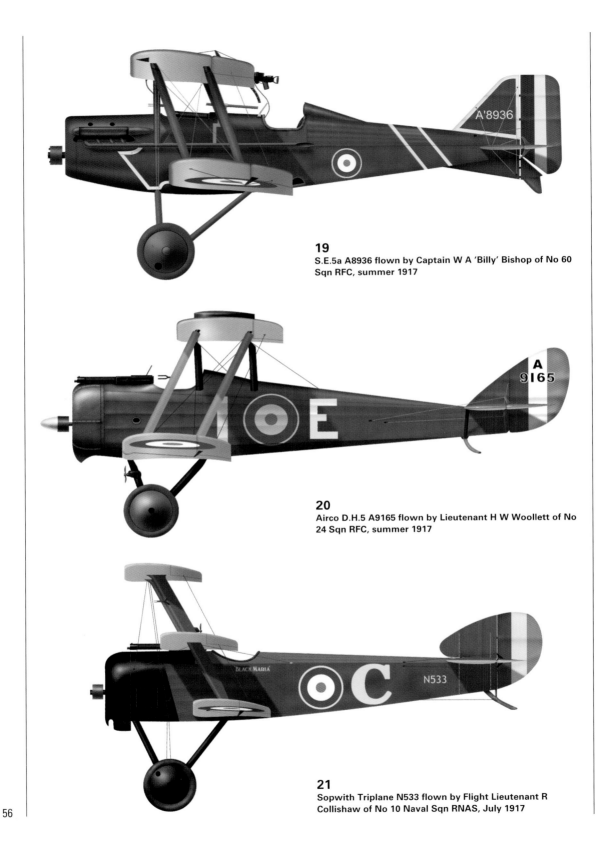

**19**
S.E.5a A8936 flown by Captain W A 'Billy' Bishop of No 60
Sqn RFC, summer 1917

**20**
Airco D.H.5 A9165 flown by Lieutenant H W Woollett of No
24 Sqn RFC, summer 1917

**21**
Sopwith Triplane N533 flown by Flight Lieutenant R
Collishaw of No 10 Naval Sqn RNAS, July 1917

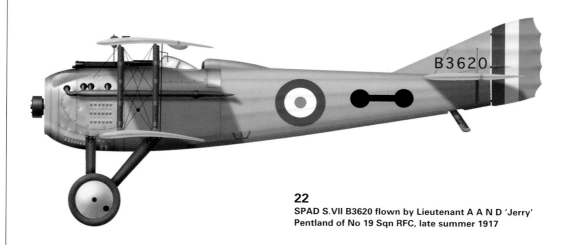

**22**
SPAD S.VII B3620 flown by Lieutenant A A N D 'Jerry'
Pentland of No 19 Sqn RFC, late summer 1917

**23**
SPAD S.VII A6662 flown by Lieutenant R A Hewat of No 19
Sqn RFC, autumn 1917

**24**
S.E.5a B4863 flown by Captain J T B McCudden of No 56
Sqn RFC, autumn 1917

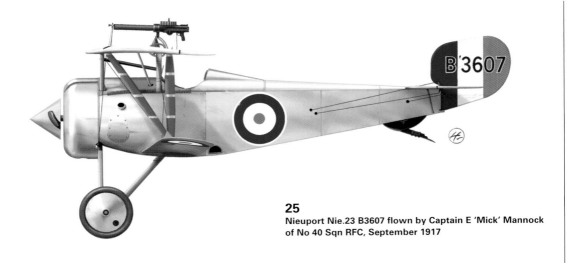

**25**
Nieuport Nie.23 B3607 flown by Captain E 'Mick' Mannock of No 40 Sqn RFC, September 1917

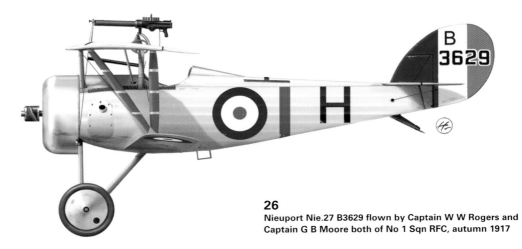

**26**
Nieuport Nie.27 B3629 flown by Captain W W Rogers and Captain G B Moore both of No 1 Sqn RFC, autumn 1917

**27**
S.E.5a B589 flown by Captain J Tudhope of No 40 Sqn RFC, winter 1917–18

**28**
Sopwith Camel B6372 flown by Captain M 'Bunty' Frew of
No 45 Squadron RFC, winter 1918

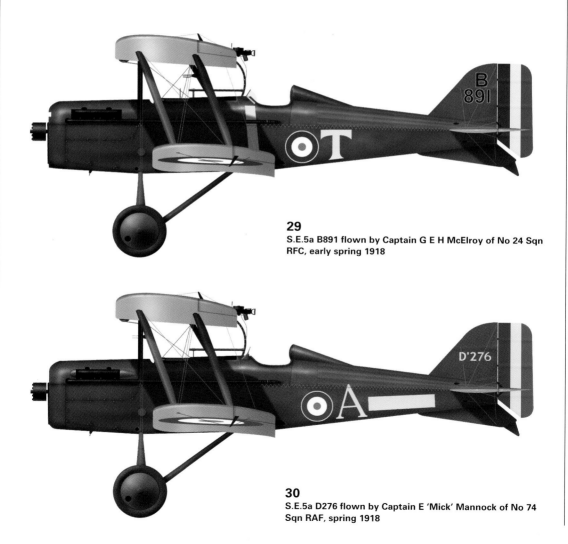

**29**
S.E.5a B891 flown by Captain G E H McElroy of No 24 Sqn
RFC, early spring 1918

**30**
S.E.5a D276 flown by Captain E 'Mick' Mannock of No 74
Sqn RAF, spring 1918

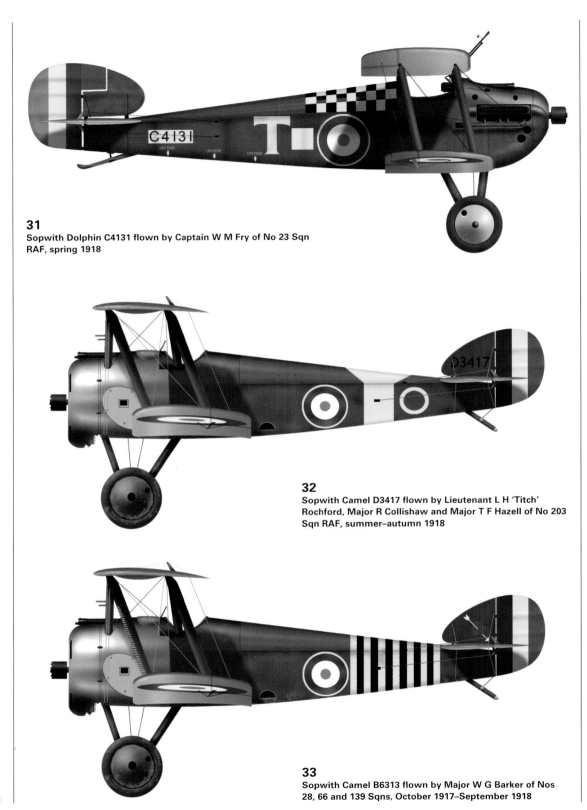

**31**
Sopwith Dolphin C4131 flown by Captain W M Fry of No 23 Sqn
RAF, spring 1918

**32**
Sopwith Camel D3417 flown by Lieutenant L H 'Titch'
Rochford, Major R Collishaw and Major T F Hazell of No 203
Sqn RAF, summer–autumn 1918

**33**
Sopwith Camel B6313 flown by Major W G Barker of Nos
28, 66 and 139 Sqns, October 1917–September 1918

**34**
Sopwith Dolphin C3879 flown by Captain R B Bannerman of
No 79 Sqn RAF, August–November 1918

**35**
Sopwith Snipe E8102 flown by Major W G Barker of No 201
Sqn RAF, October 1918

**36**
Sopwith Snipe E8050 flown by Captain E R 'Bow' King of
No 4 Sqn, Australian Flying Corps, October–November 1918

# A – Z OF ACES

T he following biographies describe the exploits of most of those pilots mentioned in the preceding chapters. They are just a few of the British and Empire aces of World War 1, but are representative of many other less well-known but nonetheless intrepid airmen who were among the first to wage war in the air.

**Captain Alfred Clayburn Atkey,** a Canadian from Minebow, Saskatchewan, was born on 16 August 1894, and was a journalist at the outbreak of war. Volunteering for the RFC, he completed his training during early 1917, then served in England with No 27 and No 28 Reserve Squadrons. In September he was posted to No 18 Squadron to fly D.H.4 bombers, but here he showed great skill, reportedly handling the big 'Four' like a Sopwith Pup. He and his various gunners claimed nine German scouts shot down between February and April 1918 whilst engaged on bombing duties. At the end of April he was posted as a flight commander to No 22 Squadron flying Bristol F.2Bs, and here he teamed up with Lieutenant C G Gass as his gunner. During May this pair claimed 27 victories including five in a day on two occasions. Two more were added on 2 June, to bring Atkey's total to 38 – the highest-scoring two-seater pilot of the war. Of these 13 and one shared were claimed destroyed, 23 and one shared out of control. Of the 29 claims made whilst the pair were flying together, 13 had been claimed to Gass's rear gun. He had claimed four other successes whilst flying with other pilots, ending the war as the RAF's top-scoring gunner. In June 1918 Atkey was posted to Home Establishment, awarded an MC and Bar; he died on 10 February 1971. Gass was also awarded an MC, and served again during World War 2 as a Squadron Leader.

**Captain Albert Ball** was born on 14 August 1896 in Nottingham. He joined the 2/7th Battalion, Sherwood Foresters, later transferring to the RFC. After training as a pilot, he joined No 13 Squadron in France in February 1916, but was posted to No 11 Squadron on 7 May. For a short period he was posted to No 8 Squadron as no single-seaters were available, but he returned to No 11, where he rapidly achieved success, gaining his first victory while flying a Bristol Scout, and then ten more flying Nieuports. Late in August, as the Somme Offensive ground to a halt, the Nieuports and their pilots were transferred to No 60 Squadron, where, by the end of September, his claims had risen to 31. He had claimed ten of these during August alone, the first time

Albert Ball ended as 10th on the list of British and Empire aces despite his early death, and was one of the few British pilots to receive much press coverage during his life. This was perhaps odd as Ball was essentially a lone flier, who preferred to stalk his quarry through cloud cover rather than become involved in multi-aircraft dogfights
*(Bruce Robertson)*

any pilot had made more than five claims in one month, while his total for September had risen to 14. These early claims included 27 aircraft and one balloon destroyed individually and one shared, five out of control and nine forced to land. He was without doubt the RFC's first really great ace, and proved an inspiration to his fellow pilots. By the time he returned to England for a rest in October, he had been awarded a DSO and Bar and an MC. After a spell as an instructor, he was appointed flight commander in the new No 56 Squadron, which took the first S.E.5s into action, arriving in France on 7 April 1917. He also had access to a Nieuport 24, with which he claimed his next victory, but thereafter he flew the S.E., rapidly claiming 11 more destroyed and one out of control to bring his total to 44, the last on 6 May 1917. The next day he was posted missing in action, after pursuing an Albatros scout over the lines in cloudy weather. For many years his fate was unknown, though the Germans subsequently credited his demise to Leutnant Lothar von Richthofen, brother of Manfred. In fact it appears that he had been pursuing von Richthofen who crash-landed, wounded. Ball was then seen by German observers to dive out of cloud and crash. He died minutes later in the arms of a young French girl. The cause of his crash has never been adequately accounted for, but does not seem to have been caused by hostile fire. He had already been recommended for a Second Bar to his DSO at the time of his death, whilst the posthumous award of the VC was announced on 8 June, this being handed to his parents by King George V on 22 July 1917.

**Captain Anthony Frederick Weatherby Beauchamp Proctor** was born on 4 September 1894 in South Africa. He left the University of Cape Town to join the Duke of Edinburgh's Own Rifles, serving in German South-West Africa. He returned to university in 1915 to complete his studies, then joining the RFC in March 1917. Late in July he was posted to No 84 Squadron which was forming with S.E.5as, going to France in September and claiming his first victory in January 1918. Only five feet two inches tall, he had to have a special seat and modified controls to allow him to fly the aircraft properly. He was awarded an MC after claiming three victories on 17 March to raise his total to nine. A Bar to his decoration followed late in May, and by mid-June he had claimed 12 aircraft and four balloons destroyed, and 12 more aircraft out of control. He returned to England for

Many of the British Empire's elements contributed signally to the British air effort in World War 1. The highest-scoring South African ace, and the winner of the VC, DSO, MC and Bar, and DFC and Bar, was Captain Anthony Weatherby Beauchamp Proctor, an officer who amassed 54 victories while serving with No 84 Squadron to rank fifth equal on the British and Empire ace list *(Bruce Robertson)*

a rest and was awarded one of the first DFCs at the start of July. He returned to the squadron in August, and in the next two months took his score to 54, including 16 balloons, the highest total of these by any pilot in the British services. He was wounded on 8 October, which caused him to be hospitalised, and on 30 November the award of a VC followed a DSO, awarded earlier in the month. He left hospital in March 1919, and after attending the RAF College at Cranwell was awarded a Permanent Commission.

He later joined No 24 Squadron, becoming a member of the squadron acrobatic team, but whilst practising on 21 June 1921 his Snipe went into a spin and crashed, and he was killed. His victories included 15 aircraft destroyed and four more shared, plus two and one shared captured and 13 and three shared balloons destroyed, and 15 and one shared out of control.

**Captain Ronald Burns Bannerman** was born in Invercargill, New Zealand, on 21 September 1890, but lived in Dunedin. He joined the RFC in March 1917 and in summer 1918 joined No 79 Squadron, which was equipped with Sopwith Dolphins. During August he claimed five aircraft and a balloon, for which he was awarded a DFC. During September he added seven more, was promoted Captain, awarded a Bar to his DFC, and then departed on leave. On his return he made four more claims, bringing his total to 17, only one of which was an out of control claim; none was shared. He remained in the RAF, becoming an Air Commodore and receiving a CBE during World War 2. He died on 2 August 1978.

**Major William George Barker** was born in Dauphin, Manitoba, on 3 November 1884. He joined the 1st Canadian Mounted Rifles in December 1914, serving in France as a machine gunner from September 1915. The following March he transferred to the RFC as an observer, joining No 9 Squadron. He was commissioned and posted to No 4 Squadron, and then to No 15 Squadron, where he made two claims as a gunner, although these were not to be included in his total. Awarded an MC, he began training as a pilot in November 1916, rejoining No 15 Squadron in his new role. He claimed a third aerial success, converted to R.E.8s and received a Bar to his MC. He was wounded by anti-aircraft fire on 7 August 1917 and returned to England, becoming an instructor. There he joined No 28 Squadron as a flight commander as it was forming, and returned to France early in October where he rapidly claimed three victories. During November the unit moved to the Italian front where he made the first three claims for the RFC by early December. Sixteen more victories followed by mid March, including five balloons on 12 February 1918. He then exchanged places with a flight commander in No 66 Squadron, taking his Camel, B6313, with him. By mid-July he had raised his total to 38, and he had received a DSO. He was then posted to command the Bristol Fighter flight in No 34 Squadron, which was being expanded into No 139 Squadron; again he was allowed to take his Camel with him. He then claimed his final eight victories in Italy with this unit, raising his total to 46. He was awarded a Bar to his DSO, also receiving the Italian Silver Medal for flying a Savoia-Pomilio S.P.4 bomber to land a spy at night behind the Austro-Hungarian lines. Camel B6313, in which he had made all his claims since October 1917, was the single most successful individual fighting aircraft in the history of the RFC/RAF. Returning to England again, Barker commanded a school of air fighting at Hounslow, but managed to arrange a brief attachment to No 201 Squadron during October, to refresh his knowledge of Western Front operations. He took with him his Sopwith Snipe E8102. On 27 October he took off to return to England, but took a last detour over the front, where he saw a two-seater, which he shot down. He was then surprised by an estimated 15 Fokker

**Captain Ronald Bannerman, a New Zealander, was a highly-successful exponent of the Sopwith Dolphin. He claimed 17 victories whilst flying these aircraft with No 79 Squadron during 1918** *(N Franks Collection)*

**Major William Barker fought in France and Italy, amassing claims for 46 victories, including nine balloons. He returned to France late in the war, and was credited with four more during his final engagement in which he was shot down and wounded. He is seen here as a pilot of a mail plane in 1919**

D.VIIs and in a fierce dogfight during which he was wounded three times, he reportedly shot down at least three of his attackers before falling himself, the whole combat being observed from the British lines. He survived to be awarded a Victoria Cross to add to his DSO and Bar, MC and two Bars, Croix de Guerre and Italian Silver Medal. He left the RAF in April 1919 and joined 'Billy' Bishop in a civil aviation venture which unfortunately failed. He then served in the new Canadian Air Force until 1924 before going into other business ventures. He became Vice President of Fairchild Aviation Corporation of Canada, but was killed in a flying accident on 12 March 1930. His total included 33 and two shared aircraft destroyed and one captured, two and seven shared balloons destroyed, and five aircraft out of control.

**Major Charles Gordon Bell** learned to fly at Brooklands in 1910, where he received Pilot's Certificate No.100 on 11 July 1911. A well-known aviator before the war, he had already flown 63 different types of aircraft by 1914. Joining the RFC late in 1914, he flew B.E.2s and Bristol Scouts in France with No 10 Squadron during 1915. He returned to England at the end of the year due to ill health, briefly taking command of the new No 41 Squadron during 1916. He did not, however, return to action, but was killed during a test flight at Villacoublay on 29 July 1918. He was remembered for his stutter, his monocle, and his ready wit. His five victories included one destroyed, two out of control and two forced to land.

**Captain Edwin Louis Benbow** was born in London on 10 December 1895. 'Lobo' as he became known, joined the Royal Field Artillery and served with a battery in France for 12 months from February 1915. He transferred to the RFC, where after a spell flying as an observer he trained as a pilot, joining No 40 Squadron during 1916. The only pilot to gain any worthwhile success whilst flying the F.E.8, he claimed six and one shared destroyed and one out of control between 20 October 1916 and 6 March 1917. On 19 March he was wounded by anti-aircraft fire, and on recovery was posted to the newly-formed No 85 Squadron as a flight commander. He returned to France with the unit in May 1918, but on 30th of that month was shot down and killed in S.E.5a C1861, the eighth victory of Oberflugmeister Schonfelder of *Jasta* 7.

**Lieutenant Colonel William Avery Bishop** was born on 8 February 1894 in Owen Sound, Ontario, Canada. He attended the Royal Military College in 1911, then joined the Canadian Mounted Rifles. Sent to France at the outbreak of war, he transferred to the RFC in July 1915, serving initially as an observer in No 21 Squadron. He sought pilot training, and in March 1917 joined No 60 Squadron to fly Nieuport Scouts. He made his first claim on 25 March, and by late July had added 35 more, 29 of them while flying B1566. He was promoted Captain in April and awarded an MC in May, followed by a DSO. He frequently flew alone, and on 2 June returned from an early morning flight, claiming to have attacked an enemy airfield and shot down three Albatros scouts which took off and attempted to intercept him, his own aircraft being shot up during the engagement. Most unusually, he was awarded a Victoria Cross for this episode purely

One of the RFC's first two aces, Major Charles Gordon Bell, claimed five victories with No 10 Squadron during 1915. He was killed whilst undertaking a test flight at Villacoublay on 29 July 1918 (*J Bruce/S Leslie Collection*)

on the basis of his own, unsubstantiated account. During July No 60 Squadron re-equipped with S.E.5s, and in one of these he added a further 11 claims in less than a month. With his total at 47, he was claimed by his Wing Headquarters to be the highest-scoring RFC pilot so far, having overtaken Albert Ball – although the RNAS Triplane pilot, Bob Little, had achieved a similar total some months earlier. In September Bishop returned to Canada on a recruiting drive, during which time he wrote his autobiography, *Winged Warfare*. He returned to England in 1918 and was given

Winner of the VC, DSO and Bar, MC, DFC, Légion d'Honneur and Croix de Guerre, William Avery Bishop was the highest-scoring Canadian ace of World War 1 with 72 victories, a figure putting him first on the list of British and Empire aces *(Bruce Robertson)*

command of No 85 Squadron, again with S.E.5as, leading this unit to France on 22 May. Between 27 May and 19 June he made a further 25 claims to bring his total to 72, all achieved whilst flying C6490 (12) and C1904 (13). The majority of his claims both in 1917 and in 1918 were made in circumstances where corroboration by witnesses was not available. Subsequently, it has proved very difficult to confirm the majority of these against German loss records. The veracity of his total has therefore been the subject of much question, culminating in a Senate Inquiry in Canada. In August 1918 Bishop joined Canadian HQ to help form the Canadian Air Force. After the war he joined W G Barker, VC, in forming a commercial aviation concern. He served with the RCAF during World War 2, becoming an Air Marshal in charge of training, and ultimately died on 11 September 1956. His total of 72 was made up of 52 and two shared destroyed, two balloons and 16 out of control.

**Captain Arthur Roy Brown** was born on 23 December 1893 in Carleton Place, Ontario. He joined the RNAS in Canada in 1915 and was posted to England in December. In May 1916 he crashed and spent three months in hospital. On recovery further illness delayed his posting to an operational unit until April 1917 when he joined No 9 Naval Squadron. He then served with Nos 11 and 4 Naval Squadrons, gaining his first victory with the former in a Sopwith Pup during July. He then rejoined No 9 Naval, now on Camels, and was awarded a DSC in October after four out of control victories. In February 1918 he became a flight commander, whilst on 1 April the unit became No 209 Squadron. On 21 April he received credit for shooting down von Richthofen, but this was his last claim, as he was then ill again. Discharged from hospital in June, he joined No 2 School of Aerial Fighting as an instructor, but crashed on 15 July after fainting in the air and was very badly injured. He spent five months in hospital, but was not declared fully fit again until five years had passed. He left the RAF in April 1919 and became an accountant in Canada. He died of a heart attack on 9 March 1944. His score of ten included two and one shared destroyed, one captured, four and two shared out of control.

**Major Keith Logan 'Grid' Caldwell** ended the war as New Zealand's top-scoring pilot. Born in Wellington on 16 October 1895, he joined the New Zealand Territorial Infantry at the outbreak of war. In August 1915 he learned to fly at a private flying club, then departed for the UK, where he joined the RFC in April 1916. In July he reached France to fly B.E.2ds with No 8 Squadron, his first victory being claimed whilst with this unit. In November he was posted to No 60 Squadron to fly scouts, remaining with this unit for nearly a year, and becoming a flight commander. During that period he claimed seven victories whilst flying Nieuport scouts, and then one after the unit had converted to the S.E.5a. Awarded an MC, he was then posted to the UK to the Special School of Flying at Gosport, and then to the Aerial Gunnery School at Ayr as an instructor. He then took command of the new No 74 Squadron which he led to France in April 1918. Here during the next seven months he made 16 more claims to raise his total to 25: 11 and two shared destroyed, one shared captured, ten and one shared out of control. He was awarded the DFC and Bar and the Belgian Croix de Guerre. Returning to New Zealand, he became a farmer, but continued to fly until World War 2. He then undertook various training and administrative duties with the Royal New Zealand Air Force, becoming AOC, RNZAF HQ in London. He left the service as an Air Commodore, CBE, and returned to farming until his death on 28 November 1980.

**Captain William Charles Campbell** was born in Bordeaux, France, on 27 April 1889, son of a Scottish father and French mother. He joined the RFC in 1916, being posted to No 1 Squadron in May 1917. Between 14th of that month and 28 July he claimed 23 victories, five of which were balloons, making him the RFC's first 'balloon-busting' ace. However, he was wounded on 31 July, and made no further claims thereafter. Awarded an MC and Bar, and then a DSO, he had been promoted flight commander. In September, on recovery from his wounds, he returned to England, spending the rest of the war as an instructor. His victories, 11 of them

No 1 Squadron contained a number of high-scoring Nieuport pilots during 1917. One of these was Captain William Campbell, who was of Franco-Scottish parentage; he was also the RFC's first balloon-busting ace, five of which were included amongst his 23 victories. He is seen here in the cockpit of a Nieuport Nie.17
*(N Franks Collection)*

claimed whilst flying Nieuport B1700, and six with Nieuport Nie.17 B3474, included 11 aircraft and five balloons destroyed, plus five aircraft and two more shared out of control.

**Major Albert Desbrisay 'Nick' Carter** was born on 2 June 1892 in Pointe de Bute, New Brunswick, Canada, and became a professional soldier, being commissioned in March 1911. He was promoted Major whilst with the infantry in February 1916, but was wounded. On recovery he transferred to the RFC, qualifying as a pilot in summer 1917. After four months of coastal patrols he was posted to France, joining No 19 Squadron where he flew SPAD S.VIIs and S.XIIIs. He became a flight commander in November and by the end of the year had claimed 15 victories, receiving a DSO in January 1918. The unit then converted to Dolphins, and with these he made 13 more claims by 16 May, ten of them in C4017, adding a Bar to his DSO. On 19 May 1918 however, he was shot down by Leutnant Paul Billik of *Jasta* 52 as the latter's 16th victory, and became a prisoner. He returned to England after the end of the war but was killed in 1919 when a Fokker D.VII he was testing broke up in the air. His total included nine and six shared destroyed, 12 and two shared out of control.

**Captain William Gordon Claxton** from Gladstone, Manitoba, was born on 1 June 1899. He volunteered for the RFC in Canada in 1917, reaching the UK later that year. In March 1918 he joined No 41 Squadron in France. First claiming in late May, he was constantly in action during the summer and had achieved 20 victories by the end of June, 13 of them in just four days, 27–30th, including six on the later date alone. He had to force-land due to damage once during that month, returning with a shot-up aircraft on two other occasions. After taking leave during July, he was awarded a DFC and became a flight commander. During late July and the first half of August he raised his total to 37, also being awarded a DSO. On 17 August 1918 he and fellow Canadian F R McCall engaged a large force of German scouts. In the ensuing dogfight Claxton was shot down by Leutnant Hans Gildmeister of *Jasta* 20, crashing in German lines. Claxton was seriously wounded in the head, but his life was saved by a skilful German surgeon and he was able to return to Canada after the war, where he became a journalist. He died on 28 September 1967. His victories included 18 and two shared destroyed, two balloons and 15 out of control.

**Captain Percy Jack Clayson** was born in Croydon, Surrey, in May 1896. He joined the RNAS on the outbreak of war, serving in France for two and a half years from December 1914. He transferred to the RFC, and at the end of October 1917 joined No 1 Squadron. He gained his first victory in mid February 1918, following which he claimed regularly and frequently until mid July, by which time he had amassed 29 victories, received an MC and a DFC, and become a flight commander. His total included nine and nine shared destroyed, one and one shared forced to land and captured, a shared balloon, plus five and three shared out of control. At the start of August 1918 he was posted to Home Establishment. He remained in the RAF after the war, flying with No 6 and No 70 Squadrons during the 1920s.

'Nick' Carter – born Albert Desbrisay – was a Canadian professional soldier who transferred to the RFC when already a Major. Flying SPADs and Dolphins with No 19 Squadron, he had claimed 28 victories before being shot down and spending the rest of the war as a PoW *(N Franks Collection)*

Captain P J Clayson was one of No 1 Squadron's successful S.E.5a pilots of 1918, claiming 29 victories with this unit between February and July of that year *(N Franks Collection via R Lynes)*

**Captain Arthur Henry Cobby,** although not the highest-scoring Australian pilot, became the top-scorer of the Australian Flying Corps. Born in Melbourne, Victoria, on 26 August 1894, he worked as a bank clerk before the war, joining the AFC in December 1916. He arrived in France with No 71 Squadron (soon to be redesignated No 4 AFC Squadron) early in 1918. He saw much action during the German Spring Offensive of 1918, claiming 29 victories in a little under six months. He was awarded a DFC and two Bars and a DSO during this period, his successes including 20 and one shared destroyed, five balloons, one aircraft captured and two out of control. Fourteen of these claims were achieved in Camel D1929, and at least eight in E1416. He served with the new Royal Australian Air Force after the war, becoming a Wing Commander in 1933. In 1936 he entered civil aviation, and also wrote his autobiography, *High Adventure.* He rejoined the service on the outbreak of World War 2, becoming an Air Commodore in 1942. He was awarded a George Medal for rescuing survivors from a crashed Catalina flying boat on 7 September 1943, and was also subsequently made a CBE. He returned to civil aviation in 1946 and died on 11 November 1955.

**Major William John Charles Kennedy Cochran-Patrick**, the son of Sir Noel Cochran-Patrick, was born in Ireland on 25 May 1896, subsequently graduating from Cambridge University. With the outbreak of war, he joined the Rifle Brigade. He transferred to the RFC early in 1915, qualifying as a pilot during April. He then became a test pilot at No 1 Aeroplane Depot, St Omer, from where on 26 April 1916 he took off in a Nieuport Scout and shot down a German two-seater, for which he was awarded an MC. He was then posted to No 70 Squadron, equipped at the time with Sopwith 1¹/₂ Strutters, claiming two further victories in these aircraft, although on each occasion his observer was killed during the action. During 1917 he became a flight commander with No 23 Squadron, now flying SPAD S.VIIs. During the spring and summer he claimed 18 further victories, becoming one of the first RFC pilots to reach a total in excess of 20; he was awarded a Bar to his MC and a DSO. In July 1917 he took command of No 60 Squadron, a role which at that time effectively precluded him from flying over the front. At the end of the year he returned to the UK to join the Training Division, but later in 1918 he returned to No 1 Aeroplane Depot. He was much involved in aerial survey work after the war, but was killed in a crash at Johannesburg, South Africa, on 27 September 1933. His victories included six and one shared destroyed, one captured, nine and one shared out of control.

**Captain Geoffrey Hornblower Cock** was born on 7 January 1896 in Shrewsbury, Salop, joining the 28th London Regiment – the Artists' Rifles OTC – in December 1915. He was seconded to the RFC in June 1916, training with No 25 Reserve Squadron. Posted to No 45 Squadron, he accompanied this unit to France on 14 October 1916. Flying Sopwith 1¹/₂ Strutters, he became a flight commander during May 1917 and was awarded an MC. He had become by far the highest-scoring pilot to fly the Strutter, claiming that he had achieved 19 victories of which he considered 15 to have been 'certain' – nine with the front gun and six with the rear. This total appears to have included a number of 'driven down' claims, which were no longer being listed by 1917, and records exist of 13 claims by him and his gunners, three and one shared destroyed and nine out of control. On 22 July 1917 he was shot down by Hauptmann Willi Reinhard of *Jasta* 11 and became a PoW. He made one abortive attempt to escape, finally being repatriated in December 1918 when the war ended. He remained in the RAF, commanding No 9 Squadron at Boscombe Down in 1935, while in 1941–42 he served on Malta during the siege of that island, subsequently retiring as a Group Captain during 1943.

**Lieutenant Colonel Raymond Collishaw,** a Canadian from Nanaimo, British Columbia, was born on 22 November 1893. A seaman before the war, he joined the RNAS in January 1916 and joined 3 Naval Wing, flying Sopwith 1$^{1}$/$_{2}$ Strutters initially. He was shot down on 27 December, but survived unhurt, being posted to No 3 Naval Squadron in February 1917 to fly Sopwith Pups, in which he made two claims to add to two made earlier with No 3 Wing. In April he joined the newly-formed No 10 Naval Squadron with Triplanes, claiming four more successes in the Dunkerque area. The unit was then posted to the Western Front, where as a flight commander he had the engine cowlings and wheel covers of all the flight's aircraft painted black, and named with the prefix 'Black'. Much of his flying over the coming months was undertaken in 'Black Maria', B5492, in which he scored 18 of the 30 victories that he claimed between 1 June and 27 July; on 6 July alone he made six claims – the first pilot to do so. He was shot down for a second time on 15 July, again surviving unscathed, but at the end of the month he was ordered home to Canada on leave, having been awarded a DSO and DSC. He returned in November 1917 and took command of No 13 Naval Squadron, flying Camels. After one victory with this unit, he moved to command No 3 Naval Squadron in January 1918, this unit becoming No 203 Squadron, RAF, on 1 April 1918. From June the unit became heavily involved in action, and by the end of September he had made 21 more claims, all in Camel D3417. He was awarded a DFC and a Bar to his DSO, finally returning to England in October to help form the new Canadian Air Force. He remained in the RAF after the war, and in 1919 led No 47 Squadron to South Russia in support of the White forces. Still flying Camels, he claimed two further victories here to bring his total to 62. During 1940–41 he commanded No 201 Group in Egypt during the early months of the Western Desert war. He then commanded No 12 Group of Fighter Command in the United Kingdom. He retired as an Air Vice Marshal in 1943 with a CB and OBE, settling in Vancouver. He died in 1976. His claims included 28 and two shared destroyed, one captured, 29 and two shared out of control.

**Major Arthur Coningham** was born in Brisbane, Australia, on 19 January 1895, but spent his early life in Wellington, New Zealand. He served with the New Zealand Expeditionary Force in Somaliland and Egypt early in the war, but was invalided out with typhoid in 1916. On recovery he made his way to England where he managed to join the RFC, and in 1917 joined No 32 Squadron, flying D.H.2s and then D.H.5s, becoming a flight commander. He claimed one victory in a D.H.2, and then nine in a single month in July 1917 with the D.H.5, making him the most

One of the leading Canadian aces, Raymond Collishaw remained in the service after World War 1, and is seen here as the station commander of RAF Bircham Newton during a visit by HM King George V and Queen Mary during May 1935. Collishaw rose to the rank of Air Vice Marshal and retired after World War 2 *(Bruce Robertson)*

successful pilot flying these aircraft. He was awarded a DSO and MC. The following year he was given command of No 92 Squadron, leading this to France after its formation with S.E.5as, and claiming four further victories during the late summer of 1918. He was twice wounded in action, once with each squadron. He remained in the RAF after the war, his initial nickname of 'Maori' deteriorating into 'Mary', by which he was known for the rest of his life. During World War 2 he enjoyed a very illustrious career, serving as AOC, Western Desert Air Force from late 1941 until early 1943. He then became AOC, 2nd Tactical Air Force until 1945, becoming an Air Marshal; he was knighted for his services. He died when an Avro Tudor of British South American Airways was lost whilst flying to Bermuda on 30 January 1948.

**Major Roderic Stanley Dallas,** an Australian, was born in Mount Stanley, Queensland, on 30 July 1891. He joined the Australian Army in 1913 and was commissioned. He attempted to transfer to the RFC soon after the outbreak of war, but was rejected, but was then accepted by the RNAS. On completion of training he joined No 1 Naval Wing at Dunkerque at the end of 1915, and by February 1917 had claimed eight victories, two of them in the prototype Sopwith Triplane, the rest whilst flying Nieuport Scouts. For this he had been awarded a DSC and promoted flight commander. Early in 1917 the Wing became No 1 Naval Squadron, fully equipped with Triplanes, and in April was attached to the RFC on the Western Front. During this month he claimed eight victories. He was awarded a Bar to his DSC, and on 14 June 1917 took command of the squadron. With the formation of the RAF on 1 April 1918 he became a Major and was posted to command No 40 Squadron on S.E.5as. On 1 June 1918 he took off alone to patrol along the front line; here he was surprised by three Fokker Triplanes of *Jasta* 14 which dived across the lines to attack him. He was shot down and killed by Leutnant Johannes Werner as the latter's sixth victory. Having added a DSO to his decorations, Dallas' final score was 33, made up of 15 destroyed, one captured, 15 and one shared out of control and one driven down. Of his 33 victories, 19 claims had been made whilst flying Triplanes, and the final nine with the S.E.5a whilst leading No 40 Squadron.

Before he was killed in a combat with three Fokker Dr I triplane fighters on 19 June 1918, Australian 'ace' Major Roderic Stanley Dallas had amassed 39 'kills' while operational with the RNAS and RAF. This photograph shows Dallas in his specially camouflaged S.E.5a, a machine later flown by G E H McElroy of the same unit *(Bruce Robertson)*

**Sergeant Ernest John Elton** was accepted for pilot training following his service with No 6 Squadron, joining No 22 Squadron early in 1918 to fly Bristol Fighters. During February and March he and his various gunners claimed 16 victories in 32 days. During his first engagement on 26 February he was shot down, but he and his gunner on that date, Sergeant C Hagan, survived unhurt. Elton remained the top-scoring NCO pilot of the RFC, and was awarded the DFM and MM, and the Italian Bronze Medal. His successes were classified as 14 destroyed and two out of control; ten of these were claimed with Elton's front gun, the other six by his rear seat gunners, with their flexible Lewis gun.

**Flight Commander Joseph Stewart Temple Fall**, was born in Millbank, British Columbia, on 17 November 1895. He joined the RNAS in 1915, initially flying Sopwith Pups with No 3 Naval Squadron late in 1916. After he had claimed eight victories (four destroyed and four out of control), the unit re-equipped with Sopwith Camels. With the new aircraft he claimed five more victories by the end of August, at which point he was promoted to Flight Commander in No 9 Naval Squadron. In this role he encouraged the members of his flight to join in his further victories, many of which were therefore claimed as shared from this time onwards. By the end of 1917 his total had increased to 36, and he had been awarded a DSC and added two Bars to this. His total included 11 individual and 12 shared aircraft destroyed, plus ten individual and three shared out of control. He returned to England as an instructor for the rest of the war, remaining in the RAF thereafter. He became a Wing Commander in 1936 and a Group Captain in 1940; he retired in 1945 and returned to his native Canada. He died there on 1 December 1988, aged 93.

One of the notable Canadian pilots of the RNAS, Flight Commander Joe Fall claimed 36 victories flying Sopwith Pups and Camels with Nos 3 and 9 Naval Squadrons. Postwar he enjoyed a successful career in the RAF. He is seen here with a Camel in the background
*(N Franks Collection)*

**Captain Matthew Brown 'Bunty' Frew** was born in Rutherglen, Scotland, on 7 April 1895. He joined the Highland Light Infantry in 1914, serving in France from January 1915–March 1916. He then transferred to the RFC, joining No 45 Squadron in April 1917, where he initially flew Sopwith 1½ Strutters. He had claimed his first five victories on these by the late summer, when the unit converted to Camels. By the end of the year his total stood at 16 when the unit moved to Italy, and here he claimed seven more by early February. However, on 15 January his aircraft had been hit by anti-aircraft fire, and in getting it down he had displaced his neck. This injury resulted in his return to England a month later, where he became an instructor at CFS. He was awarded a DSO, MC and Bar and the Italian Silver Medal He remained in the RAF, serving in Kurdistan, 1931–32, where he added a Bar to his DSO. He later commanded Nos 111 and 10 Squadrons. A Group Captain at the outbreak of World War 2, he

Hands in pockets, legs akimbo, seems to have been a favoured pose for pilots of World War 1! This is Captain Matthew 'Bunty' Frew, a successful Sopwith Camel pilot with No 45 Squadron in Italy. His 23 victories included five whilst flying Sopwith 1½ Strutters earlier in the war in France however. He retired as an Air Vice Marshal in 1948
*(N Franks Collection)*

Captain Philip Fletcher Fullard flew with No 1 Squadron, and was awarded the DSO, MC and Bar, and AFC. Fullard gained all his 40 victories in the eight months before November 1917, when he injured a leg so badly while playing football on his airfield that he was an invalid for the rest of the war, although he returned to service after it *(Bruce Robertson)*

retired in 1948 as Air Vice Marshal Sir Matthew Frew, KBE, CB, DSO, MC, AFC. His total included 12 and two shared destroyed, and nine out of control. He retired to South Africa where he died in May 1974.

**Captain Philip Fletcher Fullard** was born on 27 June 1897 in Hatfield, Hertfordshire. Educated in Norwich, he excelled at sport, playing centre half for Norwich City Football Club during 1914. He served with the Royal Fusiliers during 1915, but learned to fly at his own expense, transferring to the RFC in 1916. After training, he instructed at Central Flying School until late April 1917, when he joined No 1 Squadron in France to fly Nieuport Scouts. During a very active period between May and November, he was promoted flight commander during June, and was awarded an MC and Bar and a DSO. Despite several narrow escapes, he was never to be shot down, and on 15 November 1917 claimed his 40th victory, becoming the RFC's top-scoring Nieuport pilot of the war. Two days later he broke his leg whilst playing football, and this took a long time to heal properly, so that he was not declared fully fit again until September 1918. He did not return to the front, but did remain in the RAF, reaching the rank of Air Commodore in 1941, when be became AOC, No 246 Group. Awarded a CBE and AFC for his later services, he retired at the end of World War 2, and died on 24 April 1984. With No 1 Squadron his most successful aircraft were B3459 in which he claimed 16 victories, whilst in B6789 he achieved 13 more. His total included 15 destroyed, one shared captured and 22 and two shared out of control.

**Major John Ingles Gilmour** was born in Helensburgh, Dumbartonshire, Scotland, on 28 June 1896. He transferred to the RFC from the Argyll and Sutherland Highlanders, joining No 27 Squadron early in 1916, where he flew the rather ungainly Martinsyde G.100 'Elephant'. During September 1916 he became one of the few pilots of this aircraft to gain any success in aerial combat, claiming three victories; he was awarded an MC, though this was as much for bombing operations as for his fighting exploits. Late in 1917, however, he was posted to No 65 Squadron as a flight commander, now flying Camels. Between 18 December and 3 July 1918 he made 36 more claims, receiving two Bars to his MC and a DSO. After a period off operations he was posted to Italy to command No 28 Squadron, but shortly after his arrival the war ended. His total included 24 and three shared destroyed, one captured, one balloon and ten out of control.

**Major Lanoe George Hawker** was born into a distinguished military family on 30 December 1890. He joined the Royal Engineers, transferring to the RFC just before the outbreak of war, and was posted to France with No 6 Squadron in October 1914, flying Henri Farmans. The unit converted to B.E.2cs, and he undertook a lone bombing raid on some Zeppelin sheds, for which he was awarded a DSO. In 1915 the unit received some Bristol Scouts and F.E.2s, and he became engaged in aerial fighting in these aircraft, as has been described. During July 1915 he claimed three successes whilst flying Bristol Scouts, adding three more in August in F.E.2b 4227. On 7 September, once more in a Bristol Scout, he made his seventh and last claim, his total including one aircraft captured, three destroyed, one out of control and two forced to land. Posted back to England after the award of the Victoria Cross, he was promoted Major and formed No 24 Squadron, the RFC's first single-seater fighting scout unit, equipped with D.H.2 'pushers'. He led this unit to France in February 1916, where on 23 November he was shot down and killed by Freiherr Manfred von Richthofen, who was flying a superior Albatros D.II aircraft.

**Major Tom Falcon Hazell,** an Irishman from Galway, was born on 7 August 1892. He attended the University of London until 1910, and joined the Southern Irish Horse in September 1914, being commissioned the following month in the 7th Battalion, Royal Inniskilling Fusiliers. He served in France until 1916 when he transferred to the RFC, joining No 1 Squadron at the end of that year. In the period March–August 1917 he claimed 20 victories, becoming a flight commander and receiving an MC. He then became an instructor at the Central Flying School in England until June 1918, when he joined No 24 Squadron, again as a flight commander. Flying S.E.5as with this unit he claimed 23 further victories, including ten balloons, being awarded a DSO, and a DFC and Bar. In October 1918 he was posted to command No 203 Squadron on Camels, but the war ended before he could achieve any further success. Awarded a Permanent Commission in the new RAF, he joined No 1 Canadian Wing in 1919, serving with No 123 Squadron. He subsequently commanded Nos 45, 55, 111 and 60 Squadrons, but retired from the service in 1927. He died in Ireland in 1946. His total included 17 and one shared aircraft destroyed, eight and two shared balloons, one aircraft captured, and 11 and three shared out of control. Of his first 20 victories whilst flying Nieuport Scouts, 11 were achieved in B3455; with the S.E.5a, nine of his claims were made in E1388.

**Captain Reginald Theodore Carlos Hoidge** was born in Toronto on 28 July 1894. He transferred from the Canadian Royal Garrison Artillery to the RFC, joining No 56 Squadron in 1917 before its departure for France with the first S.E.5s. He remained with the unit until early November 1917, claiming 27 victories by the end of October, becoming a flight commander, and receiving an MC. He then became an instructor for a year, returning to the front during the autumn of 1918 as a flight commander with 1 Squadron. With this unit he added one further victory late in October, the pilot of which was seen to bale out. He died in New York City on 1 March 1963. His total was made up of seven and one shared destroyed, plus 18 and two shared out of control.

**Captain Louis Fleeming Jenkin** was born in London in 1895. He transferred to the RFC from the 9th Loyal North Lancashire Regiment,

One of the first British airmen to gain national fame, Major Lanoe George Hawker was a pioneering fighter pilot who on 24 August 1915 was awarded the VC for an action on 25 July of the same year. Flying a Bristol Scout biplane of No 6 Squadron, Hawker used the Lewis gun mounted on the starboard side of the fuselage to force down a German two-seater, then to drive down another German two-seater, and finally to shoot down in flames an Albatros two-seater. On 23 November 1916 Hawker was killed as he became the 11th confirmed victim of Manfred von Richthofen *(Bruce Robertson)*

Tom Falcon Hazell claimed 20 victories with No 1 Squadron during 1917, then becoming an instructor. In 1918 he returned to France to add a further 23 to his total (which included 10 balloons) whilst flying S.E.5as with No 24 Squadron *(N Franks Collection)*

joining No 1 Squadron on 15 May 1917 to fly Nieuport Scouts. By the end of July he had claimed 20 victories, and he was awarded an MC in August. On 11 September 1917 he made his 22nd claim, but later that day was reported missing – the same date on which the French ace Georges Guynemer was lost. Jenkin had been shot down in B3635 over Bixshoote and killed by Oberleutnant Otto Schmidt of *Jasta* 29, the eighth of this pilot's 20 victories. Jenkin's total of 22 included eight and two shared destroyed, 11 and one shared out of control; 16 of these claims had been made while flying Nieuport B1547.

**Lieutenant Alan Jerrard** was born on 3 December 1897, transferring from the 5th South Staffordshire Regiment to the RFC in 1915. In 1917 he joined No 19 Squadron, but was injured on 5 August when he crashed a SPAD. On recovery he joined No 66 Squadron in Italy in February 1918, where he claimed four victories in a month. On 30 March with two other pilots he engaged a two-seater and four scouts, then more scouts, reported to number up to 19, but now known to have been five or six strong, joined the fray and Jerrard was shot down. The other British pilots, claiming three shot down between them, returned to report that Jerrard had accounted for three before being brought down to become a prisoner. On the basis of their report he was awarded a Victoria Cross. Jerrard reported on his return after the war that he had attacked an airfield, used all his ammunition, and then been shot down. He made no claim for any hostile aircraft shot down, although three had been credited to him, bringing his total to seven. He had been shot down by the Austrian ace, Benno Fiala von Fernbrugg, commander of *Flik* 51J. Jerrard escaped late in 1918, reaching Allied lines. Also awarded the Italian Bronze Medal for Valour, he served in Russia during 1919, remaining in the RAF for some years. He died on 14 May 1968. The seven victories credited to him included one destroyed, one balloon and one out of control which he had claimed, plus the three erroneously reported destroyed on 30 March 1918.

**Captain James Ira Thomas 'Taffy' Jones** was born in St Clears near Carmarthen, South Wales, on 18 April 1896. A clerk before the war, he joined the Territorial Army in 1913, training as a wireless operator at the outbreak of war and then joining the RFC, where he served initially as an Air Mechanic on wireless duties with No 10 Squadron. Posted to France in July 1915, he undertook some flights as an observer. In May whilst at a wireless receiving station at the front he rescued two wounded gunners when their battery was under fire, being awarded an MM and the Russian Medal of St George. In October 1916 he became an observer formally, flying in B.E.2s, and in May 1917 returned to England to be commissioned and to train as a pilot. He became a member of the new No 74 Squadron in 'Mick' Mannock's flight, going to France with the unit at the end of March 1918. Between 5 May and 7 August he made 37 claims, being promoted flight commander in June and receiving a DSO, MC, DFC and Bar. His total included 28 and one shared destroyed, one balloon and six aircraft plus one shared out of control. He gained no further victories during the last three months of the war. He then volunteered for service in North Russia during 1919, but saw no action

On 30 March 1918 Lieutenant A Jerrard of No. 66 Squadron, a unit equipped with the Sopwith Camel fighter and at the time deployed on the Italian Front, was one of three No 66 Squadron pilots attacked by the Hansa-Brandenburg D. I (Ph) fighters of *Flik* 51J under the command of the redoubtable Benno Fiala, who ended the war with some 29 victories. Jerrard was separated from his comrades and attacked by several Austro-Hungarian fighters, his Camel succumbing to Fiala's guns. Jerrard managed to keep some control over his aeroplane as it crash-landed, received only minor injuries and was later awarded the VC *(Bruce Robertson)*

there. He was awarded a permanent commission, serving with the RAF until June 1936. Recalled in August 1939 as a Group Captain, he commanded a fighter operational training unit for much of the war, undertaking some operational flying in Spitfires. He died on 30 August 1960 after falling off a ladder.

**Captain Elwyn Roy 'Bow' King** was born in Bathurst, New South Wales, on 13 May 1894. He joined the Australian Light Horse, but subsequently transferred to the AFC, and was posted to No 4 AFC Squadron in France to fly Sopwith Camels. Between 20 May and 2 October 1918, he claimed 19 victories including four balloons, and was promoted to command a flight. During October the unit re-equipped with Sopwith Snipes, and with these he made seven more claims, becoming the most successful pilot of these new fighters. These claims included three Fokker D.VIIs on 30 October and two more on 4 November. He was awarded a DSO and DFC. He returned to his pre-war motor engineering business after the war, but rejoined the RAAF during World War 2, during which he died whilst commanding Point Cook airfield on 28 November 1941.

**Captain Samuel Marcus Kinkead** was born in Johannesburg, South Africa, on 25 February 1897. He joined the RNAS in September 1915 and was posted to No 3 Naval Wing in the Dardanelles, where he claimed three victories during 1916 flying Bristol and Nieuport Scouts. Posted back to England, where he had trained, he joined No 1 Naval Squadron, seeing action on the Somme and Ypres fronts, claiming six more victories

At a presentation near Nieppe Château on 6 August 1918, HM King George V talks to Captain J Ira T Jones, who on the morning of that day had brought down his 36th and 37th aircraft. A pilot of Nos 10 and 74 Squadrons, Jones ended the war with a tally of 37 victories, putting him 14th on the list of British and Empire aces. On Jones's right is Captain B Roxburgh-Smith (16 victories) and on his left Captain S Carlin (11 victories) who had a wooden leg and was nicknamed 'Timbertoes' *(Bruce Robertson)*

Having claimed around 35 victories in the Dardanelles and France during 1916–18, South African Captain Sam Kinkead flew in Russia in 1919, where he was the RAF's most successful Camel pilot. He later became a member of the RAF Schneider Trophy team, but was killed whilst testing the S.5 seaplane in 1928. He is seen here in the cockpit of his No 201 Squadron Camel during 1918
(*N Franks Collection*)

in Nieuport N5465. In mid November 1917 the unit received Camels; by the end of the year his total had reached 14 and he had been rested. He returned to the unit early in 1918, claiming a further 19 victories by mid August, adding a DFC and Bar to his earlier DSC and Bar. In 1919 he went to Russia with No 47 Squadron, flying with that unit's Camel flight, and here he claimed at least three further victories, raising his total to 36; however, it is possible that he made additional claims in Russia, his total here possibly having reached eight or ten. He was awarded a DSO for his service at this time. In 1921 he became a flight commander in No 30 Squadron, serving in Mesopotamia and Kurdistan, while later he was chosen as a member of the RAF Schneider Trophy Team. He was killed when he crashed in the Supermarine S.5 racing seaplane during a practice flight on 12 March 1928. His victories included at least five and two shared destroyed, one captured, plus 21 and three shared out of control.

**Captain Robert Alexander Little** was born in Melbourne, Australia, on 19 July 1895. He joined the RNAS in 1915, commencing operational flying from Eastchurch in January 1916. He was posted to Dunkerque in June, where initially he flew Bristol Scouts, and then undertook bombing raids in Sopwith 1½ Strutters. In October he joined No 8 Naval Squadron, claiming his first four victories with this unit flying Sopwith Pups, receiving a DSC. The unit then re-equipped with Triplanes, and he claimed a further 24 victories between April–July 1917 whilst flying these machines; 20 of these were achieved in N5493. During July Camels were received, and within two days he had made his first claim in one of these, adding ten victories by the end of July to bring his total to 38. He was awarded a DSO and Bar and a Bar to his DSC, but saw no further action until March 1918. By then he had been posted as a flight commander to No 3 Naval Squadron, which became No 203 Squadron, RAF, on 1 April. A further nine claims followed, the last of these on 22 May. On 27 May 1918 he took off at night to intercept a Gotha bomber, but when the two aircraft were illuminated by a searchlight beam, a bullet – either from his opponent or from the ground – passed through both his thighs. He crash-landed near Noeux but bled to death from his wounds. His 47 victories were the highest number claimed by any Australian and

This Albatros D.V fighter was forced down near Marceuil by Captain F R McCall, at the time a pilot of No 13 Squadron flying a Royal Aircraft Factory two-seat R.E.8 (*Bruce Robertson*)

included 17 and five shared destroyed, one and one shared captured, 21 and two shared out of control; he is also believed to have made a number of additional claims for aircraft forced to land or driven down during the early months of his time at the front.

**Captain Frederick Robert Gordon McCall** was born in Vernon, British Columbia, on 4 December 1896. During February 1916 he joined the 175th Battalion of the Alberta Regiment, and when this unit was posted to France eight months later he had already been promoted Sergeant. He was commissioned, and in March 1917 transferred to the RFC. After training, he reached France in December to join No 13 Squadron on R.E.8s, he and his observer, Lieutenant F C Farrington, claiming three German aircraft shot down during the first three months of 1918. McCall was awarded an MC and Bar for this achievement. At the end of April he was posted to No 41 Squadron to become a scout pilot, flying S.E.5as. By the end of June he had claimed 17 further victories, five of them on 30 June alone. More successes followed during July and August, his 35th and last claim occurring on 17 August when he and Captain W G Claxton engaged a large force of enemy scouts. During this fight Claxton was shot down, wounded, and taken prisoner. Immediately thereafter McCall was taken ill and evacuated to England. Awarded a DSO and DFC, he was sent home to Canada on sick leave, and was still there when the war ended. Leaving the service, he established an air transport business in his home country. He died on 2 January 1949. His total included 16 and four shared destroyed, one forced down and captured, 11 and three shared out of control.

**Major James Thomas Byford McCudden** was born in Gillingham, Kent, on 28 March 1895, one of six children, three of whom would fly with the RFC, he and his brother John both becoming aces. He joined the Royal Engineers as a bugler in 1910, transferring to the RFC as a mechanic in 1913. He went to France with No 3 Squadron in 1914, where he occasionally flew as an observer, being awarded an MM. In January 1916 he returned to England to become a pilot, returning in July to join No 20 Squadron, flying F.E.2s. Next month he moved to No 29 Squadron on D.H.2s, claiming five victories on these aircraft by mid February 1917, receiving an MC. He then became an instructor, but twice had the opportunity to fly in action with No 66 Squadron, making two further claims. In August he joined No 56 Squadron as a flight commander, where he was extremely successful, both on offensive patrols

Photographed with his dog 'Bruiser' at Turnberry in Scotland, James McCudden was only 22 at the time of his death but was the most highly decorated pilot of the Royal Flying Corps, Royal Naval Air Service and Royal Air Force in World War 1 (*Bruce Robertson*)

and whilst intercepting high-flying German reconnaissance two-seaters. By the end of February 1918 he had brought his total of claims to 57, which included 40 two-seaters since joining No 56, 21 of which fell within Allied lines; 32 of his claims were made whilst flying S.E.5a B4891. This was the top-scoring S.E.5a, in which 34 claims would be made before it was damaged in a crash on 21 March 1918. He was awarded a VC, DSO and Bar and a Bar to his MC. He returned to England to become an instructor again until July, when he departed to take command of No 60 Squadron. En route his aircraft crashed as he was taking off from Auxi-le-Château, and he was killed. His total included 27 and one shared destroyed, 19 captured, eight and two shared out of control.

**Captain George Edward Henry McElroy,** from Donnybrook, near Dublin, was born on 14 May 1893. He served with the Royal Irish Regiment, being commissioned in May 1915, but was badly gassed and was sent home on garrison duty. He managed to transfer to the RFC in February 1917, joining No 40 Squadron in France to fly Nieuport Scouts. When the unit re-equipped with S.E.5as he gained his first victory on 28 December 1917, adding ten more during January and February 1918. He was posted as a flight commander to No 24 Squadron, claiming 16 more by early April, receiving an MC and two Bars. On 7 April, after claiming three victories, he crashed into a tree on landing and was badly shaken. In June, on recovery, he rejoined No 40 Squadron, claiming 21 more victories, 17 of them during July alone. On the last day of the month 'McIrish' McElroy shot down a two-seater, but was then shot down by anti-aircraft fire and crashed to his death. His 46 victories included 26 and two shared destroyed, two and one shared balloons and 15 out of control. His most successful aircraft had been C8869 in which he claimed 17 of his total whilst with No 40 Squadron.

Posing by the radiator of a Royal Aircraft Factory S.E.5a of No. 40 Squadron are Captains G H Lewis (12 victories) and (right) George Edward Henry McElroy. Born in Ireland, McElroy was lost on 31 July 1918 after achieving 46 victories to put him in ninth equal position on the British and Empire ace list (*Bruce Robsrtson*)

Captain Andrew Edward McKeever poses at Shoreham in Kent with a captured example of the phenomenal Fokker D.VII fighter (*Bruce Robertson*)

**Lieutenant Clifford Mackay 'Black Mike' McEwen** was born in Griswold, Manitoba on 2 July 1897, and was a graduate of the University of Saskatchewan before joining the Canadian Army in March 1916. He transferred to the RFC in June 1917, and on completion of training joined the new No 28 Squadron. He served with this unit on the Italian Front until the end of the war, claiming 27 victories: 21 and two shared destroyed and four out of control. He was awarded an MC, DFC and Italian Bronze Medal for Valour. After the war he joined the new Royal Canadian Air Force, and rose to the rank of Air Vice Marshal during World War 2. In January 1944 he became AOC, 6 (Canadian) Bomber Group, where Air Chief Marshal Sir Arthur Harris considered he had turned the poorest Group into the best. He died in Toronto on 6 August 1967.

**Lieutenant Colonel Andrew Edward McKeever** was born in Listowel, Ontario, on 21 August 1895. He served in France during 1915–16 with the Canadian Expeditionary Force before transferring to the RFC in December 1916. He joined No 11 Squadron in May 1917 as the unit was re-equipping with Bristol F.2B Fighters, flying these aircraft in action with several rear seat gunners, the most frequent of whom was Sergeant L F Powell. On 7 July he and Powell claimed three victories, again claiming three on 5 August. By early September when he was awarded an MC, McKeever had 12 to his credit. Six more followed that month and eight in October, a Bar to the MC following. On 30 November 1917 they made four claims, McKeever then being awarded a DSO, and Powell a DCM. With 31 victories, McKeever was the highest scoring Bristol Fighter pilot of the war. In January 1918 he returned to England, where he formed and commanded No 1 Squadron, Canadian Air Force, just before the end of the war. In 1919 he became aerodrome manager at Mineola Field in the USA, but was critically injured in a car accident on 3 September, dying on Christmas Day that year. His victories included 18 destroyed and 13 out of control.

**Major Donald Roderick MacLaren** was a Canadian of Scots descent, born in Ottawa on 28 May 1893. An expert marksman early in life, he joined the RFC in May 1917, becoming an instructor for some time. He arrived in England in late 1917, joining No 46 Squadron. He was in

Major D R MacLaren, a Canadian of Scots descent, is seen here (left) with Lieutenant Colonel Andrew McKeever, a fellow Canadian. Behind them are Sopwith Dolphins of the first Canadian Air Force fighter squadron to be formed – too late for the war. MacLaren claimed 54 victories with No 54 Squadron, becoming commanding officer on the eve of the war's end (*N Franks Collection*)

action throughout 1918, claiming 54 victories, 17 of them in Camel D6418, between March and October, but he then broke his leg wrestling with a friend. Awarded a DSO, MC and Bar, DFC, Croix de Guerre and made a Companion of the Legion d'Honneur; he then served with the Canadian Air Force until the late 1920s. He was subsequently involved in commercial aviation and died in July 1989. His score included 15 and six shared destroyed, one shared captured, five and one shared balloons, 18 and eight shared out of control.

**Major Edward 'Mick' Mannock** was born in Aldershot, Hampshire, on 24 May 1887, the son of a serving NCO in the army. Mannock was working in Turkey as a telephone engineer at the outbreak of war and was interned as an enemy alien, but was repatriated during 1915 due to poor health. He joined the RAMC, but was commissioned in the Royal Engineers during 1916, transferring to the RFC in August of that year. In April 1917 he joined No 40 Squadron, but it was May 1917 before he was able to claim his first success. His total had risen to 15 by the end of September for which he was awarded an MC and Bar, and was promoted flight commander. The squadron then converted from Nieuports to S.E.5s in which he claimed one further victory during January 1918. He then returned to Home Establishment, where in February he was posted to the new No 74 Squadron, again as a flight commander. He returned to France with this unit at the end of March, claiming 36 more victories between 12 April and 16 June, 17 of them in S.E.5a D278. He claimed four in a day on 21 May, three in a day on two occasions and two in a day on seven occasions. Awarded a DSO and Bar, he was considered an outstanding patrol leader, and on 18 June was given command of No 85 Squadron when 'Billy' Bishop was recalled to England. He claimed seven further successes by 22 July, but on 26th of that month, having shared with his wingman in shooting down a two-seater – his 61st victory – his aircraft was hit by ground fire as he headed back low over the German lines, and he crashed to his death in flames in S.E.5a E1295, in which he had claimed all his recent successes since joining the unit. The award of a VC was not made until 18 July 1919, the citation crediting him with 59 successes. Subsequently Ira Jones, a member of his flight in No 74 Squadron, claimed that Mannock had amassed 73 victories – one more than Bishop, whom Jones clearly disapproved of, and this was accepted as his total for many years. The 61 claims which he is actually recorded as making (or in the case of the last one, was made for him) included 30 and five shared destroyed, three and two shared captured, one balloon destroyed, plus 17 and one shared aircraft out of control.

**Major Gerald Joseph Constable Maxwell** born on 8 September 1895 in Inverness, was the son of a noble Scottish Catholic family, and nephew of Lord Lovat. He was commissioned at the start of the war, seeing action at Gallipoli and in Egypt. He then returned to England, transferring to the RFC in September 1916. He joined No 56 Squadron as it was forming with the first S.E.5s, going to France in April 1917 in Albert Ball's 'A' Flight. After his initial combat he was shot down by anti-aircraft fire and crashed, but was unhurt. He was promoted flight commander late in July, and by the end of September had claimed 20 victories, being awarded an

Edward 'Mick' Mannock was a man of enormous intensity, as suggested by this photograph, and also possessed an increasingly deep hatred for the Central Powers of Germany, Austria-Hungary and Turkey *(Bruce Robertson)*

MC. He then became an instructor at the School of Aerial Fighting at Turnberry. During the summer of 1918 he requested a 'refresher' experience of operations, returning to No 56 Squadron for a five week period in June and July, during which he claimed six further victories, and received a DFC. He left the service at the end of the war, entering the Stock Exchange. He later joined the Auxiliary Air Force and was called up in World War 2, commanding Ford airfield. Ultimately he flew 167 different types of aircraft, including the Meteor jet fighter, reaching the rank of Wing Commander. His younger brother, Michael, served with No 56 Squadron during the 1939–45 war, also becoming an ace. Gerald Maxwell died on 18 December 1959. His 26 victories included ten and two shared destroyed, and eight and six shared out of control.

**Captain Thomas Percy Middleton** was born in Kew, London, on 10 May 1893. Initially he served with the 6th London Brigade of the RFA, but transferred to the RFC, joining one of the first units to operate the new Bristol F.2 A Fighter – No 48 Squadron. Arriving in France in spring 1917, he claimed seven victories with this unit by midsummer, but was then rested. He returned in April 1918 to become a flight commander in No 20 Squadron, now flying F.2Bs. During the next six months he claimed 20 further victories and was awarded a DFC. On all his successful flights with this unit he was accompanied either by Captain Frank Godfrey or Lieutenant Alfred Mills as gunner, both of whom were also awarded DFCs. Middleton's total included 20 and six shared destroyed, and one out of control. After the war he went to live in Argentina.

**Major Gilbert Ware Murlis-Green** joined the Suffolk Regiment in 1914, but a year later transferred to the RFC. Initially he flew as an observer with No 5 Squadron in France, but was then selected for pilot training. Late in 1916 he was posted to No 17 Squadron on the Salonica Front in Northern Greece, where initially he flew B.E.2ds. A month later B.E.12 fighting scouts were received, and he became involved in efforts to intercept enemy reconnaissance aircraft, for which he was awarded an MC. He achieved his first actual success on 13 December, for which a Bar was added to his MC, and by mid March 1917 his total had risen to three. He then shot down a twin-engined Friedrichshafen, adding a further victory next day, which led to the award of a DSO. With six victories on the disappointing B.E.12 to his credit, he managed to borrow a SPAD from the French, achieving his seventh success with this aircraft, and adding a Bar to his MC. Posted back to Home Establishment in England, he took command of No 44 (Home Defence) Squadron on Sopwith Camels fitted for night fighting. Flying one of these he shot down the first German aircraft to fall on British soil by night on 18 December 1917, receiving a Bar to his DSO. In June 1918 he took command of No 151 Squadron, leading this to France as the RAF's first specialised night fighting unit on the Western Front. He returned to day operations at the head of No 70 Squadron late in the war. Apart from his British decorations, he also received French and Belgian Croix de Guerre, and the Karageorge – the Serbian Order of the White Eagle. He remained in the RAF, becoming a Group Captain in 1934. His total of eight victories included four destroyed, two and one shared captured, and one out of control.

Major Gilbert Murlis-Green flew with considerable success on the difficult Salonica front during 1916–17, subsequently becoming a night fighter in defence of England, and then commanding the first night fighting unit to be posted to France. He is sitting on the wreckage of one of his early victories; he claimed 8 in all by the war's end *(N Franks Collection)*

**Major Keith Rodney Park** was born at Thames, near Auckland, New Zealand, the son of English-born parents, on 15 June 1892. He joined the New Zealand Artillery, with which he served in Egypt and at Gallipoli, being commissioned in July 1915. He then transferred to the Royal Artillery, seeing action in France with the 29th Division. He was wounded on 21 October 1916, and was invalided out of the army. Determined to continue to serve, he joined the RFC in December, and on graduating as a pilot, became an instructor. In July 1917 he joined No 48 Squadron to fly Bristol Fighters, becoming a flight commander in September and receiving an MC and Bar, and a French Croix de Guerre. During this time he was shot down twice, but survived on each occasion, claiming 17 victories by early January 1918. He was then rested for a few weeks, but returned in April to command the unit, adding three final victories to his total, which included five destroyed, plus 14 and one shared out of control. He remained in the RAF, commanding No 25 and No 111 Squadrons during the 1920s, and receiving fairly rapid promotion to Group Captain as Air Attache in Buenos Aires. During World War 2 he gained considerable fame as commander of 11 Group, Fighter Command, during the Battle of Britain, and then the defence of Malta in 1942. He ended the war as AOC-in-C in Burma. When he retired shortly after the war, he had become Air Chief Marshal Sir Keith Park, GCB, KBE, MC, DFC, DCL. He died in New Zealand on 6 February 1975.

**Captain Alexander Augustus Norman Dudley Pentland,** known as 'Jerry', was a colourful Australian, born in Queensland on 5 August 1894. He served with the 12th Australian Light Horse in Egypt and Gallipoli during 1915–16, transferring to the RFC early in the latter year. In June he was posted to France to join No 16 Squadron, flying B.E.2cs; a few days after his arrival, he and his observer shot down an attacking Fokker Eindecker. He was then posted to No 29 Squadron equipped with D.H.2s, but broke his leg playing rugby. On recovery be became an instructor until July 1917 when he joined No 19 Squadron. Now flying SPADs he claimed nine more victories before 26 September, when he crashed after his aircraft had been hit by an artillery shell, suffering some injury; he was awarded an MC. Another period of instructing followed recovery, and then in April 1918 he returned to France as a flight commander in No 87 Squadron, flying Dolphins. He claimed 13 more victories, the last two on 23 August in a fight in which he was shot down and wounded in the leg, apparently by Vizefeldwebel Knobel of *Jasta* 57; he was awarded a DFC. After the war he served with the RAAF, then becoming a commercial airline pilot. During World War 2 he commanded an air-sea rescue unit in the Pacific as a Squadron Leader. He died in 1983. His score included ten and one shared destroyed, nine and three shared out of control.

**Captain Francis Grainger Quigley** was born on 10 July 1894 in Toronto. He went to France during the spring of 1915 with the 5th Field Company, Canadian Army Engineers, but two years later transferred to the RFC, subsequently being posted to No 70 Squadron to fly Camels. His first claims were made on 10 October, and by the end of the year he had already achieved nine victories. His 33rd claim was made on

A charismatic Australian who saw action in B.E.2cs, D.H.2s, SPADs and Dolphins, 'Jerry' Pentland claimed 23 victories before being shot down and wounded by a pilot of *Jasta* 57 on 23 August 1918, whilst serving with No 87 Squadron. He survived to serve with the Royal Australian Air Force during World War 2 *(N Franks Collection)*

23 March, by which time he had claimed 15 victories in that month alone, twice claiming four in a day; all the claims during this month were made whilst flying B7475. His total then stood at 12 and eight shared aircraft destroyed, one balloon shared destroyed, plus ten and two shared out of control. Awarded a DSO, MC and Bar, and Mentioned in Despatches several times, his successes included the shooting down with two other pilots of the German ace Leutnant Walter von Bülow of *Jasta B* (28 victories) on 6 January 1918. On 27 March Quigley was wounded in the ankle during a dogfight. After convalescence, he returned to Canada to become an instructor. In September 1918 he requested a further tour in France, but whilst sailing across the Atlantic he became ill with the influenza that was sweeping Europe at the time. On arrival at Liverpool he was removed to hospital, but died two days later on 20 September 1918.

**Lieutenant Colonel Wilmot Brabazon Rees** was born in Caernavon, Wales, on 31 July 1884, and was commissioned in the Royal Garrison Artillery in 1903, and was attached to the West African Frontier Force during 1913–14. He was seconded to the RFC on 10 August 1914. He served in France as a flight commander in No 11 Squadron, claiming six victories whilst flying Vickers F.B.5 'Gun-buses', for which he was awarded an MC. In 1916 he was given command of No 32 Squadron, the third D.H.2 unit, continuing to fly over the lines as often as possible. On 1 July 1916 single-handedly attacked four German two-seaters, which were then joined by two or three more. He drove one off, forced another to land and then hit the observer of a third, forcing this down as well, although he was wounded himself; two of these successes were added to his

A high-scoring Canadian ace, Captain F G Quigley of No 70 Squadron is seen in the cockpit of a captured Pfalz D.IIIa fighter. In one sortie he shot down a German balloon and the four fighters defending it *(Bruce Robertson)*

Major L W B Rees was one of the first British fighter pilots to become well known, and won the Victoria Cross for an action on 1 July 1916 when he flew his Airco D.H.2 'pusher' fighter of No 32 Squadron into combat with six or seven German fighters and later returned to base wounded and without ammunition. Rees remained in the Royal Air Force after World War 1 and retired in 1931 with the rank of Group Captain *(Bruce Robertson)*

Seen in the cockpit of his Royal Aircraft Factory S.E.5a is A P F Rhys Davids, the ace of No 56 Squadron who was credited with the September 1917 shooting down of Leutnant Werner Voss, the 48-victory ace who led *Jagdstaffel* 10 and was fourth on the overall German ace list *(Bruce Robertson)*

existing total to bring his score to eight, and he was awarded a VC for the 1 July action. He then commanded the Air Fighting School at Ayr for the rest of the war. He remained in the RAF, retiring as a Group Captain in 1931, having added an OBE and an AFC to his awards. His victories included one captured, one destroyed, one forced to land and seven driven down.

**Lieutenant Arthur Percival Foley Rhys Davids** was born on 27 September 1897. He attended Eton College, where he became Head Boy, obtaining a scholarship to Oxford, which he had to postpone taking up because of the war. He joined the RFC in 1916 and was subsequently posted to No 56 Squadron, accompanying this unit to France with the first S.E.5s in April 1917. He survived being attacked by the German ace, Lieutenant Kurt Wolff of *Jasta* 11, during the fight from which Albert Ball failed to return, and by the end of May had made six claims. In June the unit returned to England to defend London, returning to France in July, flying S.E.5as. On 23 September he and a number of the unit's other leading pilots engaged one of the two leading German aces of the time, Lieutenant Werner Voss, whom Rhys Davids finally shot down after a long, hard fight. He then also brought down Leutnant Karl Menckhoff who had himself nearly shot down Rhys Davids on 14 September. He was awarded an MC and Bar, followed in October by a DSO. He claimed his 25th victory on 11 October, but on 27th, leading 'B' Flight into a dogfight, he failed to return. He had been shot down and killed by Leutnant Karl Gallwitz of *Jasta* Boelcke. His total included four and two shared destroyed, two captured, 14 and three shared out of control.

**Captain Herbert Victor Rowley,** born on 24 October 1897, joined the RNAS in June 1916, being posted to No 1 Naval Squadron in February 1917. He claimed five victories whilst flying Triplanes and four more in a Camel by April 1918. During World War 2 he served as an Air Commodore in the India-Burma theatre.

**Captain Benjamin 'Dad' Roxburgh-Smith** gained his nickname due to being considerably older than most of the young pilots with whom he served. Before the war he had worked as a bank clerk, and was a married man with a family, living in Bromley, Surrey. He joined the RFC and, after training, was posted to No 60 Squadron during 1917. Before he had a chance to gain any success, he crashed in a Nieuport Scout and was injured, being evacuated to England. Here he became an instructor for a time, but in 1918, now aged 34, he joined No 74 Squadron and returned to France with this new unit as a member of Captain 'Mick' Mannock's 'A' Flight. Here he claimed 22 victories by mid October, and became a flight commander, receiving the DFC and Bar and the Belgian Croix de Guerre. He was once shot down, on 19 July, but survived with only slight wounds. His total included 13 and four shared destroyed and five out of control.

**Second Lieutenant Indra Lal 'Laddie' Roy** was born in Calcutta, India, and was sent to England for his education. He joined the RFC in July 1917 and after training was posted to No 56 Squadron in France at the end of October. A week later he crashed his S.E.5a, and consequently was sent back to England for further training. There he was categorised as medically unfit for further flying and it was some weeks before he was able to get this ruling cancelled. He then returned to France, joining No 40 Squadron on 19 June 1918, where he became a member of George McElroy's flight. Between 6 and 19 July he claimed ten victories – four and one shared destroyed and four and one shared out of control – but was then killed in action on 22 July when his S.E.5a, B180, in which he had claimed all his successes, was shot down in flames over Carvin during a dogfight with Fokker D VIIs of *Jasta* 29. The award of a DFC was subsequently gazetted in September for the man who had become India's first – and to date, only – fighter ace, at the age of 19.

**Major Alexander MacDonald Shook** was born in Tioga, Ontario, Canada, on 2 December 1888. He served throughout 1916 with No 5 Wing, RNAS, flying Sopwith 1¹/2 Strutters. In April 1917 he joined No 4 Naval Squadron on its formation, becoming a flight commander the following month; he also claimed

Major Alexander Shook, a Canadian pilot with the RNAS and later the RAF, flew Sopwith 1¹/2 Strutters and Pups before claiming the first victories to be achieved with the new Sopwith Camel, when these were supplied to No 4 Naval Squadron in May 1917. He is seen here in one of these aircraft in which he brought his personal total to 12 *(J Bruce/S Leslie Collection)*

three victories flying Sopwith Pup N6200. At the end of May the unit received the first Sopwith Camels, and he made his first claims in one of these aircraft, N6347, on 5 June. Awarded a DSC in August, he made his eighth claim on 21 October 1917, but was wounded on this date. He returned to the unit early in January 1918, remaining until mid-April, by which time he had made four more claims. He was awarded a DSO and Croix de Guerre. He became a Major in the new RAF and was later awarded an AFC. He died in Ontario on 30 May 1966. His 12 victories included six and one shared destroyed, and five out of control.

**Captain Frederick James Harry Thayre** was born in London on 20 October 1893. He transferred to the RFC early in the war, qualifying as a pilot in July 1915. He served initially with No 16 Squadron during 1916, flying B.E.s, in one of which he and his observer claimed a victory during March. He was later posted to No 20 Squadron where he flew F.E.2ds with Lieutenant (later Captain) Francis Cubbon as his gunner. After an initial two victories during April 1917, the pair added no less than 15 during May, both being awarded the MC and Bar. On 3 May, after forcing a German two-seater to land, they fought off 26 Albatros Scouts, exhausting all their ammunition and resorting finally to their pistols to continue firing! Two more claims in early June brought their total together to 19, Thayre personally having now been involved in 20 victories and Cubbon in 21, making him at the time the RFC's top-scoring observer/gunner. On 9 June 1917 however, the F.E. in which they had achieved all their successes, A6430, suffered a direct hit from anti-aircraft battery K Flak 60 near Warneton, and both were killed. Thayre's total of 20 included 17 and one shared destroyed and two out of control.

Captain John Lightfoot Trollope gained fame when he claimed six victories in a single day on 24 March 1918. Four days later, having brought his total to 18, he was shot down and wounded, becoming a PoW. His left hand was amputated in a German hospital, and he eventually lost his arm
(N Franks Collection)

**Captain John Lightfoot Trollope** was born in Wallington, Surrey, on 30 May 1897. He served as a despatch rider in 1915, but transferred to the RFC during that year. Initially he flew Sopwith 1½ Strutters with No 70 Squadron, but gained no successes. Late in 1917 he was posted to No 43 Squadron as a flight commander, during the first three months of 1918 claiming 18 victories flying Camels with this unit, including six on 24 March and three on 28th, receiving an MC. On the latter date he was shot down in C8270, in which he had claimed all but five of his victories, by Leutnant Paul Billik of *Jasta* 52, and was taken prisoner, having been wounded in his left hand; the hand was amputated in a German hospital. He was medically repatriated in June 1918, to find that he had been awarded a Bar to his MC. However his wound continued to give him much trouble and eventually his arm had to be amputated at the shoulder. During World War 2 he served as a Wing Commander with Maintenance Command. His total included 11 and one shared destroyed, one captured, one balloon and four out of control.

**Captain Arthur Whitehair 'Wiggy' Vigers** was born on 20 January 1890; he saw early service with the Royal Engineers, receiving an MC and being Mentioned in Despatches during 1915. Seconded to the RFC, be flew as an observer with No 15 Squadron until 1917, when he was selected for pilot training. He joined No 87 Squadron in April 1918 to fly Dolphins, remaining with the unit until 1919. During this time he was awarded a DFC, promoted to flight commander and Mentioned in Despatches again. He claimed 14 victories, including six destroyed plus seven and one shared out of control. He emigrated to Australia after the war, where he served in the RAAF; he died in September 1968.

**Lieutenant Colonel Alan Machin Wilkinson** was born in Eastbourne, Sussex, on 21 November 1891. After attending Oxford University, he joined the Hampshire Regiment of the Territorial Force. With the outbreak of war he transferred to the RFC, joining No 24 Squadron on 16 January 1916 and accompanying this unit to France during the spring. Here he adapted his D.H.2 to carry two Lewis guns, rapidly becoming the unit's most successful pilot, with ten victories by the end of August 1916, and a flight commander. Awarded a DSO during October, he returned to England that month, where he was posted to No 48 Squadron as it was forming on Bristol F.2A Fighters. Again he became a very successful early exponent of this aircraft when it was first exposed to action over the Western Front, and with his various gunners he claimed nine victories during April 1917, seven of them in the course of just four days – four in one day. He was awarded a Bar to his DSO, but in May was promoted to command No 23 Squadron on SPAD S.VIIs. Administrative duties here prevented him from flying often, and he was to make no further claims. He later commanded No 8 Aerial Fighting School until 1919. His 19 victories included six and two shared destroyed, six and four shared out of control and one forced to land.

Lieutenant Colonal Alan Wilkinson, mistakenly identified in the past as a Canadian, was the most successful pilot of the Airco D.H.2 with No 24 Squadron in 1916, where he claimed 10 victories. Subsequently a flight commander in No 48 Squadron, he added 9 more successes whilst flying the early F.2A version of the Bristol Fighter – four of them in one day *(N Franks Collection)*

**Captain Henry Winslow Woollett** from Southwold, Suffolk, was a medical student when war broke out. He at once joined the Lincolnshire Regiment, taking part in the Suvla Bay landings in the Dardanelles in 1915. He transferred to the RFC in 1916, joining No 24 Squadron in France in November. He claimed one victory in a D.H.2 during April 1917, and then four more in D.H.5 A9165 during the summer, becoming a flight commander and receiving an MC. He then returned to England as an instructor until March 1918, when he joined No 43 Squadron. During the next five months he claimed 30 more victories, 11 of them balloons – the second highest total of these opponents in the British service. Awarded a DSO, a Bar to his MC, a Croix de Guerre and the Legion d'Honneur, he was posted home during August to command three training squadrons. He remained in the RAF serving in Iraq in 1924 and commanding No 23 Squadron during 1930–31. He died on 31 October 1969. Apart from the balloons, his total included 20 aircraft destroyed, six of them in one day, and four out of control. Twenty-three of his claims were made whilst flying Camel D6402.

# APPENDICES

## APPENDIX 1

### Aces Who Claimed 20 or More Victories

(including 'driven-down' or 'out of control', balloons and 'shared')

| | | | | | | |
|---|---|---|---|---|---|---|
| Lt Col W A Bishop | C | 72 | | Capt W McK.Thomson | C | 26 |
| Lt Col R Collishaw | C | 62 | | Maj K L Caldwell | NZ | 25 |
| Maj E Mannock | Br | 61 | | Maj R J O Compston | Br | 25 |
| Maj J T B McCudden | Br | 57 | | Lt A P F Rhys Davids | Br | 25 |
| Capt A F W Beauchamp Proctor | SA | 54 | | Capt S W Rosevear | C | 25 |
| Maj D R MacLaren | C | 54 | | Lt H G E Luchford | Br | 24 |
| Maj W G Barker | C | 50 | | Capt W E Shields | C | 24 |
| Capt R A Little | A | 47 | | Capt J A Slater | Br | 24 |
| Capt G E H McElroy | I | 46 | | Capt W M Alexander | C | 23 |
| Capt A Ball | Br | 44 | | Capt W C Campbell | Br | 23 |
| Maj T F Hazell | I | 43 | | Capt M B Frew | Br | 23 |
| Capt P F Fullard | Br | 40 | | Capt C F King | Br | 23 |
| Maj J I Gilmour | Br | 39 | | Capt H P Lale | Br | 23 |
| Capt W L Jordan | Br | 39 | | Capt A A N D Pentland | A | 23 |
| Capt A C Atkey | C | 38 | | Capt H A Whistler | Br | 23 |
| Capt E D Claxton | C | 37 | | Capt P Carpenter | Br | 22 |
| Capt J I T Jones | Br | 37 | | Capt T S Harrison | SA | 22 |
| Lt C M McEwen | C | 37 | | Capt L F Jenkin | Br | 22 |
| Flt Cdr. J S T Fall | C | 36 | | Capt J Leacroft | Br | 22 |
| Capt S M Kinkead | SA | 35-40 | | Catp B Roxburgh-Smith | Br | 22 |
| Capt F R G McCall | C | 35 | | Capt J L M White | C | 22 |
| Capt H W Woollett | Br | 35 | | Maj W J C K Cochran-Patrick | I | 21 |
| Capt F G Quigley | C | 33 | | Capt C R R Hickey | C | 21 |
| Maj G H Bowman | Br | 32 | | Capt R A Maybery | Br | 21 |
| Maj R S Dallas | A | 32 | | Capt E J K McCloughrey | A | 21 |
| Lt Col A E McKeever | C | 31 | | Flt Lt R P Minifie | A | 21 |
| Capt S F H Thompson | Br | 30 | | Capt G E Thomson | Br | 21 |
| Maj C D Booker | Br | 29 | | Lt L M Barlow | Br | 20 |
| Capt P J Clayson | Br | 29 | | Capt D J Bell | SA | 20 |
| Capt A H Cobby | A | 29 | | Ltd K B Conn | C | 20 |
| Capt L H Rochford | Br | 29 | | Capt E C Johnston | A | 20 |
| Maj A D Carter | C | 28 | | Capt C H P Lagesse | Br | 20 |
| Capt J E Gurdon | Br | 28 | | Capt I D R McDonald | Br | 20 |
| Capt R T C Hoidge | C | 28 | | Maj K R Park | NZ | 20 |
| Capt D Latimer | I | 28 | | Capt C G Ross | SA | 20 |
| Capt T P Middleton | Br | 27 | | Capt W A Southey | SA | 20 |
| Capt F O Soden | Br | 27 | | Capt F J H Thayre | Br | 20 |
| Capt A T Whealy | C | 27 | | | | |
| Capt W J F Harvey | Br | 26 | | | | |
| Capt E R King | A | 26 | | | | |
| Maj G J C Maxwell | Br | 26 | | | | |
| Capt W E Staton | Br | 26 | | | | |

n.b. A = Australian (8); Br = British (38 – English, Scottish and Welsh); C = Canadian (21); I = Irish (4); NZ = New Zealand (2), SA = South African (6)

## Adjustment A: Claims For Aircraft And Balloons Destroyed Or Captured

| | | | |
|---|---|---|---|
| Lt Col W A Bishop | 56 (2 shared) | Maj D R MacLaren | 28 (8 shared) |
| Maj J T B McCudden | 47 (1 shared) | Capt A H Cobby | 27 (1 shared) |
| Maj W G Barker | 45 (9 shared) | Capt R A Little | 24 (6 shared) |
| Maj E Mannock | 41 (7 shared) | Flt Cdr J S T Fall | 23 (12 shared) |
| Capt A F W Beauchamp Proctor | 38 (8 shared) | Lt. C M McEwen | 23 (2 shared) |
| Capt G E H McElroy | 31 (3 shared) | Capt E D Claxton | 22 (2 shared) |
| Capt H W Woollett | 31 | Capt P J Clayson | 21 (11 shared) |
| Capt J I T Jones | 30 (1 shared) | Capt F R G McCall | 21 (4 shared) |
| Capt A Ball | 29 (1 shared) | Capt F G Quigley | 21 (9 shared) |
| Lt Col R Collishaw | 29 (1 shared) | Capt E R King | 20 (3 shared) |
| Maj J I Gilmour | 29 (3 shared) | Capt E J K McCloughrey | 20 |
| Maj T F Hazell | 29 (3 shared) | Capt T P Middleton | 20 |

## Adjustment B: Claims For Aircraft Excluding Balloons Destroyed Or Captured

| | | | |
|---|---|---|---|
| Lt Col W A Bishop | 54 (2 shared) | Lt C M McEwen | 23 (2 shared) |
| Maj J T B McCudden | 47 (1 shared) | Capt A F W Beauchamp Proctor | 22 (5 shared) |
| Maj E Mannock | 40 (7 shared) | Capt E D Claxton | 22 (2 shared) |
| Maj W G Barker | 36 (2 shared) | Capt A H Cobby | 22 (1 shared) |
| Lt Col R Collishaw | 29 (1 shared) | Maj D R MacLaren | 22 (7 shared) |
| Capt J I T Jones | 29 (1 shared) | Capt F R G McCall | 21 (4 shared) |
| Capt A Ball | 28 (1 shared) | Capt P J Clayson | 20 (10 shared) |
| Maj J I Gilmour | 28 (3 shared) | Capt T P Middleton | 20 |
| Capt G E H McElroy | 28 (2 shared) | Capt F G Quigley | 20 (8 shared) |
| Capt R A Little | 24 (6 shared) | Capt H W Woollett | 20 |
| Flt Cdr J S T Fall | 23 (12 shared) | | |

# APPENDIX 2

## Order of Battle

### 1 Royal Flying Corps, Summer 1916

| Unit | Aircraft | Airfield |
|---|---|---|
| 1 Squadron | Nieuport 17, Morane Biplane and Parasol, Martinsyde S1 | Bailleul |
| 11 Squadron | Vickers F.B.5, Nieuport 13, Bristol Scout D | Savy |
| 20 Squadron | F.E.2b | Clairmarais |
| 22 Squadron | F.E.2b | Bertangles |
| 23 Squadron | F.E.2b | Le Hameau |
| 24 Squadron | D.H.2 | Bertangles |
| 25 Squadron | F.E.2b, Bristol Scout D | Lozingham |
| 27 Squadron | Martinsyde G.100 | Fienvillers |
| 29 Squadron | D.H.2, Nieuport 16 | Abeele |
| 32 Squadron | D.H.2 | Treizennes |
| 60 Squadron | Morane Type N, Morane Type BB | Vert Galant |
| 70 Squadron | Sopwith 1½ Strutters | Fienvillers |

### Royal Flying Corps, Summer 1917

| Unit | Aircraft | Airfield |
|---|---|---|
| 1 Squadron | Nieuport 17 | Bailleul |
| 11 Squadron | Bristol F.2.B | La Bellevue |
| 19 Squadron | SPAD S.VII | Estrée Blanche |
| 20 Squadron | F.E.2d | Boisdinghem |
| 22 Squadron | F.E.2b | Le Hameau |
| 23 Squadron | SPAD S.VII | La Lovie |

| | | |
|---|---|---|
| 24 Squadron | D.H.5 | Baizieux |
| 27 Squadron | Martinsyde G.100 | Clairmarais |
| 29 Squadron | Nieuport 17 | Poperinghe |
| 32 Squadron | D.H.5 | Droglandt |
| 40 Squadron | Nieuport 17 | Bruay |
| 41 Squadron | D.H.5 | Lealvillers |
| 43 Squadron | Sopwith 1½ Strutter | Auchel |
| 45 Squadron | Sopwith Camel | St Marie-Cappel |
| 46 Squadron | Sopwith Pup | Bruay and Sutton's Farm* |
| 48 Squadron | Bristol F.2B | Bray Dunes |
| 54 Squadron | Sopwith Pup | Leffrinckhoucke |
| 56 Squadron | S.E.5/5a | Estrée Blanche |
| 60 Squadron | Nieuport 17/S.E.5 | Le Hameau |
| 66 Squadron | Sopwith Pup | Estrée Blanche |
| 70 Squadron | Sopwith Camel | Estrée Blanche |

* temporarily detached for Home Defence duties

## Royal Naval Air Service

| Unit | Aircraft | Airfield |
|---|---|---|
| 1 (N) Squadron | Sopwith Triplane | Bailleul |
| 3 (N) Squadron | Sopwith Camel | Furnes |
| 4 (N) Squadron | Sopwith Camel | Bray Dunes |
| 6 (N) Squadron | Sopwith Camel | Bray Dunes |
| 8 (N) Squadron | Sopwith Triplane/Camel | Mont St Eloi |
| 9 (N) Squadron | Sopwith Triplane/Camel | Leffrinckhoucke |
| 10(N) Squadron | Sopwith Triplane | Droglandt |
| Seaplane Defence Flight | Sopwith Pup | St Pol |

## Royal Air Force Scout Units, Autumn 1918

### Western Front

| Unit | Aircraft | Airfield |
|---|---|---|
| 1 Squadron | S.E.5a | Bouvincourt |
| 3 Squadron | Camel | Lechelle |
| 11 Squadron | F.2B | Mory |
| 19 Squadron | Dolphin | Abscon |
| 20 Squadron | F.2B | Iris Farm |
| 22 Squadron | F.2B | Aniche |
| 23 Squadron | Dolphin | Bertry E. |
| 24 Squadron | S.E.5a | Busigny |
| 29 Squadron | S.E.5a | Marcke |
| 32 Squadron | S.E.5a | Pronville |
| 39 Squadron | F.2B | Bavichove |
| 40 Squadron | S.E.5 | Aniche |
| 41 Squadron | S.E.5a | Holluin E. |
| 43 Squadron | Snipe | Bouvincourt |
| 46 Squadron | Camel | Busigny |
| 48 Squadron | F.2B | Reckem |
| 54 Squadron | Camel | Merchin |
| 56 Squadron | S.E.5a | La Targette |
| 60 Squadron | S.E.5a | Quiery |
| 62 Squadron | F.2B | Villers-les-Cagnicourt |
| 64 Squadron | S.E.5a | Aniche |
| 65 Squadron | Camel | Bisseghem |
| 70 Squadron | Camel | Droglandt N |

| 73 Squadron | Camel | Malencourt |
| 74 Squadron | S.E.5a | Marcke |
| 79 Squadron | Dolphin | Reckem |
| 80 Squadron | Camel | Bertry W. |
| 84 Squadron | S.E.5 | Bertry |
| 85 Squadron | S.E.5 | Escaucourt |
| 87 Squadron | Dolphin | Soncamp |
| 88 Squadron | F.2B | Bersee |
| 92 Squadron | S.E.5a | Berty E. |
| 94 Squadron | S.E.5a | Senlis |
| 151 Squadron | Camel (NF) | Bancourt |
| 152 Squadron | Camel (NF) | Carvin |
| 201 Squadron | Camel | La Targette |
| 203 Squadron | Camel | Bruille |
| 204 Squadron | Camel | Heule |
| 208 Squadron | Snipe | Maretz |
| 209 Squadron | Camel | Bruille |
| 210 Squadron | Camel | Boussieres |
| 213 Squadron | Camel | Bergues |
| 2 ACF Squadron | S.E.5a | Auchel |
| 4 ACF Squadron | S.E.5a | Auchel |

## Independent Air Force

| 43 Squadron | Camel | Bettancourt |

## Italy

| 28 Squadron | Camel | Treviso |
| 66 Squadron | Camel | San Pietro |
| 139 Squadron | F.2B | Grossa |

## Middle East/Mediterranean

| 72 Squadron | SPAD S.VII, S.E.5a, M.1C, G.100 | Baghdad, Mesopotamia |
| 111 Squadron | S.E.5a | Kantara, Palestine |
| 145 Squadron | S.E.5a | Ramleh, Palestine |
| 150 Squadron | M.1C, S.E.5a, Camel | Kirce, Salonica |
| 222 Squadron | Camel    (one flight) | Thasos, Greece |
| 1 AFC Squadron | F.2B | Haifa, Palestine |

## Home Defence

| 33 Squadron | Avro 504 (NF) | Kirton-in-Lindsay |
| 36 Squadron | F.2B | Usworth |
| 44 Squadron | Camel | Hainault Farm |
| 50 Squadron | Camel | Bekesbourne |
| 51 Squadron | Camel | Marham |
| 61 Squadron | S.E.5a, Camel | Rochford |
| 76 Squadron | F.2B | Ripon |
| 77 Squadron | Avro 504 (NF) | Penston |
| 78 Squadron | Camel | Sutton's Farm |
| 90 Squadron | Avro 504 (NF) | Buckminster |
| 112 Squadron | Camel | Throwley |
| 141 Squadron | F.2B | Biggin Hill |
| 143 Squadron | Camel | Detling |

## 1

**Airco D.H.2 flown by Major L G Hawker of No 24 Sqn RFC, 1916**

The RFC's first ace, Lanoe Hawker had already claimed his final victory when he was asked to form No 24 Squadron, the RFC's first single-seater fighting scout unit, equipped with D.H.2 'pushers'. All Hawker's claims had been in other types of aircraft.

## 2

**Bristol Scout 5312 flown by Lieutenant Albert Ball of No 11 Sqn RFC, May 1916**

Albert Ball was posted to No 11 Squadron on 7 May 1916. Nine days later on 16 May, he claimed the first of his 44 victories whilst flying this Bristol Scout over the Givenchy-Beaumont area.

## 3

**SPAD S.VII A.253 flown by Captain E L Foot of No 60 Sqn RFC, September 1916**

Having claimed three victories with No 11 Squadron in Royal Aircraft Factory F.E.2bs, Captain Foot made the fourth of his five claims on 28 September in A.253, one of the first SPAD S.VIIs available to the RFC, when he attacked an Albatros two seater over Avesnes les Bapaume.

## 4

**Sopwith Pup N5182 flown by Captain R A Little of No 8 Naval Sqn RNAS, late 1916**

Australian-born Robert Little made his first three claims in this Sopwith Pup during November and December 1916. With a final tally of 47 victories, he was the highest scoring Australian ace of the war.

## 5

**S.E.5 A4850 flown by Captain Albert Ball of No 56 Sqn RFC, April 1917**

No 56 Squadron was the first to take the new Royal Aircraft Factory S.E.5 Scout into action, arriving in France on 7 April 1917. Albert Ball claimed 11 of his 44 victories flying S.E.5s with No 56 Squadron. The first four of these occurred during April 1917 in this aircraft: A4850.

## 6

**SPAD S.VII B.1524 flown by Captain W J C K Cochran-Patrick of No 23 Sqn RFC, April 1917**

Irish-born ace William Cochran-Patrick had already claimed three victories before he became a flight commander with No 23 Squadron early in 1917. During that spring and summer he added a further 18 claims, three of which were made whilst flying B.1524 during April 1917.

## 7

**S.E.5 A4863 flown by Lieutenant G G C Maxwell of No 56 Sqn RFC, April 1917**

Lieutenant, later Major, Gerald Maxwell joined No 56 Squadron as it was being formed and flew the new S.E.5 Scout in Albert Ball's 'A' flight. He claimed the first of his 26 victories in A4863 on 24 April.

## 8

**S.E.5 A4862 flown by Lieutenant R T C Hoidge of No 15 Sqn RFC, early summer 1917**

Lieutenant Hoidge, a Canadian, was another future ace who flew with No 56 Squadron when it arrived in France in April 1917. He claimed the first eight of his 28 victories whilst flying. All but one of his total were achieved when serving with this unit.

## 9

**Nieuport Nie.17 B1566 flown by Captain W A 'Billy' Bishop of No 60 Sqn RFC, 1917**

The legendary but controversial Victoria Cross winner, William A 'Billy' Bishop made 29 of his 72 claims whilst flying B1566 with No 60 Squadron between April and July 1917. Bishop, a Canadian, was the highest-scoring British and Empire ace of the war.

## 10

**SPAD S.VII B.1537 flown by Lieutenant J M Child of No 19 Sqn RFC, May 1917**

Lieutenant Child made his first two claims with No 19 Squadron whilst flying SPAD S.VII B.1537: an Albatros two seater near Douai on 27 April and an Albatros D.III on 25 May. Child accumulated eight claims by the end of the war.

## 11

**S.E.5 A4868 flown by Lieutenant A P F Rhys Davids of No 56 Sqn RFC, May 1917**

Arthur Rhys Davids, victor over the great German ace, Werner Voss, claimed the first six of his 25 victories in A4868 during May 1917. Rhys Davids was eventually shot down and killed by Leutnant Karl Gallwitz of *Jasta* Boelcke on 27 October 1917.

## 12

**SPAD S.VII A6663 flown by Lieutenant A H Orlebar of No 19 Sqn RFC, early summer 1917**

Lieutenant Orlebar, later a member of the Schneider Trophy Team, claimed his first two victories with No 19 Squadron in A6663, both Albatros D.IIIs, on 23 May and 5 June. He later added five more whilst flying Camels with No 43 Squadron.

## 13

**Sopwith Triplane N5493 flown by Captain R A Little of No 8 Naval Sqn RNAS, July 1917**

Robert Little had claimed his first four victories flying Sopwith Pups. He then transferred to

Triplanes. By July 1917 he had claimed 24 Triplane victories of which 20 were achieved flying N5493, his second machine.

## 14

### Nieuport Nie.17 B1506 flown by Lieutenant A W B Miller of No 29 Sqn RFC, early summer 1917

Archie Miller claimed all his six victories in B1506 between 1 June and 12 July 1917. His individual number was '6' and he was in 'C' flight, hence the large 6C painted on the side of the fuselage. He was shot down and killed in this aircraft on 13 July by Leutnant Hans Adam of *Jasta* 6.

## 15

### Sopwith Triplane N5487 flown by Sub Lieutenant W H Alexander of No 10 Naval Sqn, RNAS, early summer 1917

Sub Lieutenant Alexander, a Canadian member of No 10 Naval Squadron's 'Black Flight', claimed all his eight Sopwith Triplane victories during June–July 1917 in N5487. He then added 15 more when flying Camels.

## 16

### Bristol F.2B Fighter F4336 flown by Captain A E McKeever

Andrew McKeever was the most successful exponent of the Bristol F.2B Fighter. From June to November 1917 he claimed 31 victories whilst serving with No 11 Squadron RFC. F4336 appears to have been an aircraft which he flew later in the war, after his departure from the front line.

## 17

### Nieuport Nie.17 B3459 flown by Captain P F Fullard of No 1 Sqn RFC, summer 1917

By the time Philip Fullard took over B3459 he had already claimed 11 victories and claimed a further 16 in this machine between 17 July and 22 August 1917. He claimed his 40th victory on 15 November 1917 to become the RFC's top scoring Nieuport pilot of the war.

## 18

### Nieuport Nie.17 B3474 flown by Captain W C Campbell of No 1 Sq RFC, summer 1917

Another of No 1 Squadron's successful Nieuport pilots of 1917, and the RFC's first 'balloon-busting' ace, was William Campbell, who claimed 23 victories between May and July 1917. The last six of these were achieved in B3474.

## 19

### S.E.5a A8936 flown by Captain W A 'Billy' Bishop of No 60 Sqn RFC, summer 1917

'Billy' Bishop began flying the S.E.5a with No 60 Squadron during summer 1917. He claimed 11 victories in A8936 during July and August before returning to the UK with his total at 47.

## 20

### Airco D.H.5 A9165 flown by Lieutenant H W Woollett of No 24 Sqn RFC, summer 1917

Henry Woollett had already claimed one victory in a D.H.2 in April before claiming his second–fifth victories in A9165 during July and August 1917. He claimed a further 30 victories flying with No 43 Squadron in 1918.

## 21

### Sopwith Triplane N533 flown by Flight Lieutenant R Collishaw of No 10 Naval Sqn RNAS, July 1917

Raymond Collishaw claimed 34 victories whilst flying Sopwith Triplanes with No 10 Naval Squadron, where he led his famous 'Black Flight' of Canadians. His last two Triplane claims were made in N533 on 27 July 1917.

## 22

### SPAD S.VII B3620 flown by Lieutenant A A N D 'Jerry' Pentland of No 19 Sqn RFC, late summer 1917

After one victory flying a B.E.2c, Australian Lieutenant 'Jerry' Pentland claimed nine victories flying SPADs with No 19 Squadron, seven of them in B3620 during August and September 1917. On 26 September his aircraft was hit and Pentland was wounded by an artillery shell. He recovered, returning to France in 1918 to claim a further 13, finishing the war with a grand total of 23.

## 23

### SPAD S.VII A6662 flown by Lieutenant R A Hewat of No 19 Sqn RFC, autumn 1917

Canadian Richard Hewat claimed his first three of six victories with No 19 Squadron whilst flying A6662 during September and October 1917, although he was wounded in the head by machine gun fire on 26 October. His last three claims were in Sopwith Dolphins.

## 24

### S.E.5a B4863 flown by Captain J T B McCudden of No 56 Sqn RFC, autumn 1917

Arguably the RFC's greatest ace, James McCudden became an ace in February 1917 flying D.H.2s. He went on to claim 50 of his 57 victories flying S.E.5as with No 56 Squadron, including 40 two-seaters, 21 of which fell within Allied lines. Of these, nine were achieved in B4863 during September and October 1917.

## 25

### Nieuport Nie.23 B3607 flown by Captain E 'Mick' Mannock of No 40 Sqn RFC, September 1917

As late as September 1917 Edward 'Mick' Mannock was still flying in Nieuport Scouts and after a slow start had achieved a score of nine. During the month he claimed five more victories in B3607, plus one in another machine.

He was killed in action on 26 July 1918 with a final score of 61 claims.

## 26
### Nieuport Nie.27 B3629 flown by Captain W W Rogers and Captain G B Moore both of No 1 Sqn RFC, autumn 1917
Wendall Rogers, a Canadian, made two of his ten claims in B3629 during October 1917, whilst fellow Canadian Guy Moore gained his sixth and seventh victories with it in December 1917 and January 1918. He then added three more when flying S.E.5as.

## 27
### S.E.5a B589 flown by Captain J Tudhope of No 40 Sqn RFC, winter 1917–18
Captain John Tudhope, a South African pilot in No 40 Squadron, claimed six of his ten victories in B589 during the period December 1917 to March 1918.

## 28
### Sopwith Camel B6372 flown by Captain M 'Bunty' Frew of No 45 Squadron RFC, winter 1918
Having joined No 45 Squadron in April 1917, Matthew 'Bunty' Frew claimed his first five victories on Sopwith 1 1/2 Strutters before transferring to Camels. 'Bunty' Frew flew Camel B6372 in Italy with No 45 Squadron, claiming the last seven of his 23 victories with this aircraft during January and February 1918.

## 29
### S.E.5a B891 flown by Captain G E H McElroy of No 24 Sqn RFC, early spring 1918
Dubliner George McElroy claimed 46 victories flying with No 24 and No 40 Squadrons, all achieved in S.E.5as between December 1917 and July 1918. Five of these were gained in B891 with No 24 Squadron during February and March 1918.

## 30
### S.E.5a D276 flown by Captain E 'Mick' Mannock of No 74 Sqn RAF, spring 1918
Edward 'Mick' Mannock, already with a score of 16 under his belt, returned to the front in April 1918 as a flight commander in No 74 Squadron. He claimed 17 of his 36 victories scored between 12 April and 16 June when flying D276, including four in a day on 21 May.

## 31
### Sopwith Dolphin C4131 flown by Captain W M Fry of No 23 Sqn RAF, spring 1918
Captain Fry had already claimed nine victories flying Nieuports and SPADs by mid January 1918 when No 23 Squadron re-equipped with Sopwith Dolphins. He made two further claims in this new type, the second in C4131 on 11 May 1918.

## 32
### Sopwith Camel D3417 flown by Lieutenant L H 'Titch' Rochford, Major R Collishaw and Major T F Hazell of No 203 Sqn RAF, summer–autumn 1918
Camel D3417 enjoyed a distinguished career with No 203 Squadron during 1918. First it was flown by 'Titch' Rochford, who claimed his 20th and 21st victories in it early in June. It was then taken over by Raymond Collishaw who claimed the final 19 of his 60 World War 1 victories with it by September. Finally it was flown by Tom Hazell when he became commanding officer of the unit in October.

## 33
### Sopwith Camel B6313 flown by Major W G Barker of Nos 28, 66 and 139 Sqns, October 1917–September 1918
The greatest Camel of them all was B6313 which William Barker flew in France and Italy from October 1917 to September 1918. After initial service with No 28 Squadron, this aircraft accompanied its pilot to No 66 Squadron and then to No 139 Squadron. All but four of Barker's 50 victories were claimed whilst flying this machine, making it the highest-scoring fighter of the war. By late summer 1918 the markings applied to the aircraft had obliterated the serial number, previously carried on the rear fuselage. This was the only known example of an aircraft being marked with victory tallies during the war, indicated by small white horizontal stripes painted on an interplane strut.

## 34
### Sopwith Dolphin C3879 flown by Captain R B Bannerman of No 79 Sqn RAF, August–November 1918
New Zealander Robert Bannerman, a highly successful Dolphin ace, claimed 14 of his 17 victories in C3879 between 3 August and 1 November 1918.

## 35
### Sopwith Snipe E8102 flown by Major W G Barker of No 201 Sqn RAF, October 1918
E8102 was taken to France by William Barker in October 1918 to allow the pilot a brief refresher experience of conditions there. On 27 October it was shot down in a combat during which Barker was subsequently credited with having achieved his final four victories before he fell, wounded. He was awarded a Victoria Cross in respect of this engagement.

## 36
### Sopwith Snipe E8050 flown by Captain E R 'Bow' King of No 4 Squadron, Australian Flying Corps, October–November 1918
Captain King was the most successful exponent of the Sopwith Snipe during its brief career, claiming seven victories in E8050 during late October/early November 1918 ending the war with a total of 26 victories.

# INDEX

References to illustrations are shown in **bold**. Plates are shown with page and caption locators in brackets.

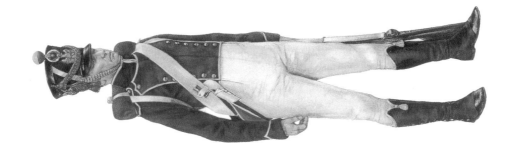

# FIND OUT MORE ABOUT OSPREY

❑ Please send me a FREE trial issue
of Osprey Military Journal

❑ Please send me the latest listing of Osprey's publications

❑ I would like to subscribe to Osprey's e-mail newsletter

Title/rank _____

Name _____

Address _____

_____

_____

Postcode/zip _____    state/country _____

e-mail _____

Which book did this card come from?

_____

❑ I am interested in military history

My preferred period of military history is _____

❑ I am interested in military aviation

My preferred period of military aviation is _____

I am interested in (please tick all that apply)

❑ general history    ❑ militaria    ❑ model making
❑ wargaming    ❑ re-enactment

Please send to:

**USA & Canada**: Osprey Direct USA, c/o Motorbooks
International, P.O. Box 1, 729 Prospect Avenue, Osceola,
WI 54020

**UK, Europe and rest of world**:
Osprey Direct UK, P.O. Box 140, Wellingborough, Northants,
NN8 2FA, United Kingdom

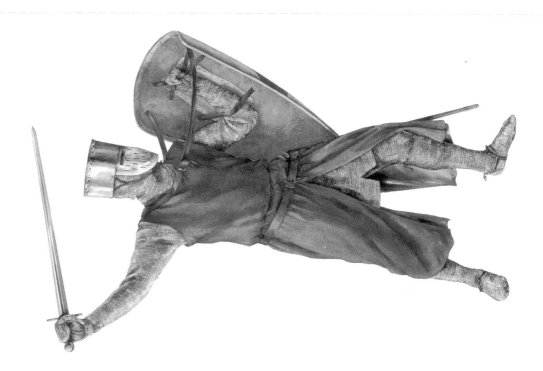

OSPREY
PUBLISHING

www.ospreypublishing.com

call our telephone hotline
for a free information pack

USA & Canada: 1-800-458-0454
UK, Europe and rest of world call:
+44 (0) 1933 443 863

**Young Guardsman**
Figure taken from *Warrior 22:*
*Imperial Guardsman 1799–1815*
Published by Osprey
Illustrated by Christa Hook

**Knight, c.1190**
Figure taken from *Warrior 1: Norman Knight 950 – 1204AD*
Published by Osprey
Illustrated by Christa Hook

POSTCARD